Winning Ways
To Make Quilts

by Connie Hester

INTERNATIONAL

95 Mayhill Street
Saddle Brook, NJ 07662

Acknowledgements:

© 1992 Connie Hester. All rights reserved. No part of this book may be reproduced, transmitted, or stored in any form or by any means, electronic or mechanical, without prior written permission from the author and the publisher.

A special thank you to the following companies for their generosity: New Home Sewing Machine Company, Fairfield Processing Corporation, Concord House, Springmaid, Peter Pan, and P & B Textiles.

Photography by CNC Photographics, 3601 East 29th, Bryan, TX.

Graphics and layout by Shimp Personalized Publication Services, Inc., Las Vegas, NV.

Published by EZ International, 95 Mayhill Street, Saddle Brook, NJ 07662.

Printed in USA.

ISBN 1-881588-01-7

Table of Contents

Table of Contents, continued

Winning Construction Tips

I am a strong advocate of doing things right the first time. Not only does this produce quality results, it avoids wasting time and materials. My compulsive nature has previously dictated techniques which, though fail-proof, took too much time, especially after the births of my two children. Faced with the prospect of never finishing another quilted project, I searched for techniques which, though faster, would not sacrifice accuracy. Unfortunately, I was not satisfied with any existing techniques for piecing triangle-blocks, which are found in nearly all pieced pattern blocks.

Illus 1.

This led to my creating SPEED GRIDS® – transparent grid stencils with laser-cut channels for marking the sewing and cutting lines on one of the two fabrics in the triangle-blocks. Marking must be done with a water-soluble marker, because, first, the marker will not shift the fabric like pencils will (it marks as it touches), and second, the channels are designed for these markers, making them too wide for accuracy with a pencil, which falls to one side of the channel. After marking on the wrong side of the first fabric, it is pinned, right sides together, to the second fabric in the triangle-blocks. The beauty of this technique is that the triangle-blocks are sewn together before cutting them apart into sewn triangle-blocks! Not only does this stabilize novelty fabrics like satins, crepe satins, rayons, knit suedecloth, and denim to produce perfect triangle-blocks, it eliminates the handling of tiny individual triangles in the ½" and 1" finished sizes and it eliminates sewing any bias edges! SPEED GRIDS® are as wonderful for piecing one single triangle-block from tiny scraps as they are for piecing hundreds at a time from yardage. Something that further pleases me is that my fabric stash is not reduced to ribbons – strips cut into all widths in anticipation of a prospective triangle-block!

SPEED GRIDS® reduce marking, cutting, and sewing time by six times! No more marking around individual triangle templates; no more cutting strips or cutting and sewing bias edges; no more inconsistent or out-of-square blocks from drawing your own grids onto the fabric. Complete instructions are included inside the SPEED GRIDS® package, but do use enough pins to stabilize the two fabrics while sewing on the diagonal lines. Remember that each triangle on the grid represents one sewn triangle-block. When using directional prints, mark half of the required triangle-blocks, then turn the SPEED GRIDS® over and mark the second half of the required triangle-blocks. This will provide mirror-imaged orientation of the directional prints. Currently, SPEED GRIDS® are available in ½", 1", 2", and 3" finished triangle-block sizes.

I now find myself breaking pattern blocks into triangle-blocks, squares, and rectangles to use

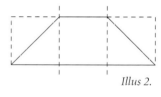

Illus 2.

SPEED GRIDS® wherever I can. For example, refer to the *Christmas Ribbons* pattern block in which I changed the trapezoid shape into two triangle-blocks and a square. Although I created more pieces, the combination of accurate rotary-cut squares and SPEED GRIDS® made it faster to piece!

Accurate piecing is critical for the balanced stretching of a quilt top when quilting it. If it is necessary to trim entire blocks and portions of blocks to the proper size, not only will seams and points not match within or between the blocks, but fabric and time are wasted and the pattern blocks will not lay flat or look square when joined to borders and sashings. Further complicating this issue is the take-up of fabric in the seams when at rest. Proper measurements are read when the pieced block is evenly stretched flat, which is very difficult to duplicate under a template.

ROTARY CUTTING

The invention of the rotary cutter has proved to be a boon to speed piecing. Using the rotary cutter, special cutting mat, and thick clear acrylic ruler, strips of fabric can be cut across the width of the fabric yardage for unpieced squares and rectangles in pattern blocks as well as for sashings and inner borders. Final borders need to be cut parallel with the selvedge to avoid rippled edges on a quilt. Accuracy may be sacrificed with a rotary cutter when too many layers of fabric are cut at once and when the acrylic ruler, almost imperceptively, scoots against the pressure of the rotary cutter. Avoid the latter by putting pressure-sensitive sandpaper on the underside of the acrylic ruler and by very carefully moving your hand down the ruler as the rotary cutter moves. When cutting pieces for miniatures, where there is no margin of error, fabrics should be cut in a single layer.

TEMPLATES

Trace most patterns onto clear template material with a fine tip permanent marker. The center of a drawn line is the most accurate line to follow. Cut out templates on the inside edge of the marked line to allow for the pencil line markings around the template on the fabric. Quarter-inch seam allowances are included in each piecing pattern template in this book, unless otherwise noted. All applique patterns need ⅛-¼" seam allowances added "by eye" when cutting out the marked shapes from the fabric. I mark around pattern templates with a mechanical pencil since the lead is so thin. On dark fabrics, I use a #914 Cream Berol Prismacolor pencil which needs to be sharpened often due to the soft lead.

Drawing my appliqué and quilting designs onto vellum or tracing paper, I rely heavily on a light table in a number of situations. First, it is more reliable for tracing appliqué and quilting motifs onto the quilt top than taping them to a window. Second, it is much easier and does not depend upon daylight. Third, it is more accurate for tracing these designs onto pattern blocks, again because there is no distortion from sagging on the window. Fourth, it is more convenient for individual appliqué pieces, regardless of size. Fifth, whether appliquéing or piecing, I can simply trace them directly onto the fabric when the template would be used only one time! For appliqué, lay both the pattern and the fabric right sides *up* on the light table, and trace. For piecing, lay both the pattern and the fabric right sides *down* on the light table, and trace. Add seam allowances before cutting.

A light table can be a topless table frame covered with glass or a 3' x 4' piece of plexi-glass, balanced on the end of an ironing board, with a 100-watt lamp (minus the shade) standing underneath on the floor.

When drawing/designing your own templates, especially those too large to fit on a sketch pad, it is very useful to remember two formulas for finding the lengths of the sides of a right triangle when two of the sides are equal:

Diagonal B =
Side A x 1.414
Side A =
Diagonal B x .707

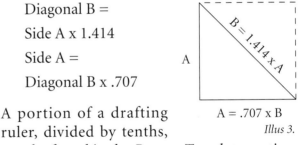

A = .707 x B

Illus 3.

A portion of a drafting ruler, divided by tenths, may be found in the *Pattern Templates* section.

FABRIC

Always pre-wash and press your fabrics. Through bitter experience, I have found that pre-washing first in a sink of warm water is a must to see if any fading is going to occur. Sometimes repeated rinsings are needed before the color stops running. This cannot be seen in a washing machine. If the fading does not stop, I do not use that fabric in a quilt. If it does stop running, I put it through a complete warm water cycle of the washing machine, dry it, and press it, as needed. Always trim the selvedges from the fabric before marking or cutting. The selvedge puckers the fabric, so accuracy may be at risk. Use tightly woven 100% fabrics. Loosely woven fabrics allow batting to migrate through them. If a looser weave must be used for some special effect, line each piece with a tighter weave, then sew as if they are one fabric.

Always mark or set aside the longest and the largest pieces from the fabric to be sure there will be enough when needed. When using fabric which has not had every square inch committed to a project, I routinely limit myself to 20" of the 40+" width, so I will always have enough for quilt borders on the straight of the grain. All yardage requirements for each pattern in this book are based upon 41" of usable fabric between selvedges.

Consider the scale of the prints used, especially in miniatures, and keep everything in perspective. Plaids add a wonderful touch to pieced projects. When pieces are small, few plaid fabrics can look like many, due to different areas of the plaids being viewed. Large plaids can give the appearance of further piecing and can give simple pieced designs a more complex appearance. Plaids, in contrast to such fabrics as flowery chintzes, nondescript prints, batiks, or marbles, also contribute another dimension in mood.

MACHINE PIECING

"THINK ROWS." Always plan your piecing strategy before sewing a pattern block or a quilt top together. The easiest way to do this is to sew in straight lines with ¼" seams, from one raw edge to the other. Backstitching is not necessary unless the piece is not going to be quilted right away. With this in mind, where possible, divide the pattern block into rows or straight portions; then, where applicable,

divide these further into rows of squares and rectangles. (See pattern block piecing diagrams throughout this book.) Follow the same strategy when piecing blocks into a quilt top, whether the rows are horizontal or on the diagonal. When piecing rows on the diagonal, the triangles at the ends of each row should have diagonals on the straight of the grain (rather than the side, as is customary). This prevents distortion of the quilt top's ultimate dimensions and insures that the quilt will hang straight without ruffled edges.

An exact ¼" seam allowance throughout the pieced project is critical. The more seams included or the smaller the pieces, allowing less margin of error overall, the more important this is. It is helpful to mark ¼" on the sewing machine's throat plate if possible. I sew on a New Home sewing machine. The Memory Craft 7000 and 8000 series machines have the ¼" marked on a presser foot as well as over the bobbin case. There are also presser feet available which limit the movement of the fabric to ¼" away from the needle. If the ¼" seam allowance raw edge falls right over the feed dogs, a tape guide may be placed onto the plate over the bobbin case to guide the fabric to the needle. Although magnetic or screw-on seam guides are available, they may be rendered useless if either the presser foot or the feed dogs are too wide, so check your machine before purchasing one.

For further speed in piecing, feed pairs of pieces through the machine assembly-style fashion, butting each pair against the next pair, forming an uncut chain of sewn pairs. Take the chain to the ironing board, press open, and cut apart, saving thread as well. I use dark, medium, and light neutrals in the brown and black families rather than matching threads (these threads should never show), a #10-#11 sewing machine needle, and sew with 9-10 stitches per inch (25mm setting). If the stitches are smaller, they are harder to remove and could break down the fibers in the fabrics.

When piecing irregular shapes, such as diamond tips, to square corners, stick a pin through both the diamond tip and the corner of the square where the two ¼" seam allowances intersect each piece. DO NOT always trust that the tail sticking out beyond the square corner will line up with the ¼" seam allowances since this is not always the case. Precision piecing of odd-shaped pieces which do not line up flush with adjacent pieces demands marking seamlines; otherwise, it is difficult to find where the error exists when the pieces do not fit together.

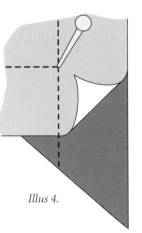

Illus 4.

There are a couple of considerations before deciding which direction to press the seam allowances. Try to press the seams toward the darker fabrics to avoid seam allowance shadows behind the lighter fabrics. For this same reason, be sure to trim the seam allowances so that the raw edges are even.

However, if a pattern block has a lot of pieces, or if piecing on a small scale, the first priority is to alternate the directions of the seam allowances from one row to the next, regardless of the lightness or darkness of the fabrics. This means that if all seam allowances in the top row press to the right, all seam allowances in the second row should press to the left, all seam allowances in the third row press to the right, and so forth. These alternating seam allowances also insure perfectly matched seams since they virtually lock themselves into exactly the right position. Points will be sharper, too, if seam allowances are pressed away from the triangle with the point. Alternating seam allowances also reduce bulk; however, if the presser foot hangs up on a seam junction, displacing the seamlines, try decreasing the presser foot pressure.

When piecing even heavy denim, top stitch each seam ¹⁄₁₆" from the pressed seam edge, then trim seam allowances close to stitching. Plan ahead in order to alternate directions of seam allowances. The pieced product will not even need to be lined! (See 5" denim *Grape Basket* block in Photo #6.)

When pressing the seam allowances, always press first from the wrong side to prevent exposing piecing threads. If needed, lightly press the right side afterwards. Be careful not to push or pull against the seam while pressing; besides exposing threads, distortion may occur. Allow to cool completely before picking it up.

APPLIQUÉ

See *Templates* section. I still prefer hand appliqué to machine appliqué because I have more control. Controlled machine appliqué requires a lot of preparation to secure the seam allowances underneath as well as skill to manipulate the sewing machine with a small hemstitch and nylon thread. I use a blind-stitch, a #10 crewel needle, and thread to match the piece to be appliquéd onto a background, and I turn under the seam allowances as I go.

BATTING

Battings vary in loft and in fiber content. I prefer "Cotton Classic" by Fairfield Processing Corp. It has an 80% cotton, 20% polyester fiber content with a low loft that encourages small quilting stitches while showing just enough relief. The drape of the finished product is unbeatable.

My sewing machine has a wonderful stitch for splicing pieces of batting together into larger batts. It is the multi-stitch zigzag. While a regular zigzag stitch scrunches up the batting, this stitch produces a smooth joint on the ¼" overlapped edges (trim excess). No splicing will be noticed by eye or by touch.

Prewashed flannel can be used for a lightweight batting if plenty of piecing covers the "top" or clothing. An 80/20 cotton batt is also an excellent lightweight batting, even when the project has no piecing. *Birds-In-Air Jumper* is an example of seam allowances concentrated enough and distributed evenly enough to substitute for any batting.

QUILTING

The quilt top, batting, and backing must be basted together enough to prevent shifting while quilting, regardless of quilting technique. When choosing a backing fabric, there are several considerations: 1) the backing should complement the quilt top; 2) a solid color will highlight quilting stitches; 3) a print will hide quilting stitches; 4) a print with a design to follow from the back will add another dimension to the quilt top; 5) a batting lighter in weight than the quilt top will produce quilting relief on the backing rather than on the quilt top; 6) double-wide, 90" fabric usually eliminates a seamline; 7) the backing may need to match the bobbin thread, if machine quilting; and 8) backing, bobbin thread, and quilt top may all need to match for some machine quilting techniques.

If the backing needs to be pieced, it should be done in a balanced manner, either with a design of its own or with simple geometric symmetry. It should be cut 2"-4" larger all around than the finished quilt size.

To baste, lay the backing right side down on a table or the floor and tape it in place. Two 4' x 8' sheets of plywood, a pingpong table, or cafeteria/library tables are helpful. Spread batting evenly over the backing; it should be the same size as the backing.

Check wrong side of the quilt top for loose dark threads before centering it over the batting, right side up. Take care not to shift seam allowances from their pressed positions.

Hand baste with ½"-1" long stitches from the center of the quilt out to the corners. Use white sewing thread to avoid thread dyes from marring the quilt top. Continue basting from the center out to the edges, between previously basted lines, keeping stitching lines 2"-4" apart. I prefer this configuration to a cross-grid because it allows some spreading of the quilt top while avoiding pleating at the basting intersections. However, I took exception to this rule when I basted *Plaids, Plaids, Plaids* vertically in order to keep plaids and seamlines from scooting while quilting a design completely unrelated to the seamlines. On small projects, I may use quilting pins – long straight pins with white ball heads. Judges complain that safety pins either leave large holes or metal residue on the quilt top, and they also get in my way when machine quilting.

When choosing a quilting design, I like to contrast a strong geometric design with something feathery or flowing, or vice-versa. I also like to quilt in the seamline "ditch" to outline/accentuate the pieced design. In sashings or borders, the quilted design should cover to within ¼" of the seamlines. Be sure to quilt in the border seamline ditch, too, or the seamline will stand out in an unattractive manner. Quilting needs to be balanced over the entire surface of the quilt, with no area larger than a clenched fist left unquilted. With this in mind, the same sort of quilting design and/or technique should be balanced over the quilted surface, also.

I mark quilting designs with a water-soluble marker, being sure to flush the marks out of the quilt when it is finished. This is the best thing I have found for ease of marking the most complex lines, for markings remaining in place until I no longer need them, and for even more easily washing out. On dark fabrics, I use a #914 Cream Berol Prismacolor pencil which is easy to rub off with a damp washcloth. Quilting designs may be traced (see *Templates*), or stencils or templates may be made for laying on top of the quilt top and marking around. Straight lines may be marked with drafting tape, which also provides a sharp edge against which to quilt, but beginners should beware of diagonal grids over large areas/borders since a missed point is quite noticeable. Remember, the diagonal of a square does not divide evenly into most borders unless planned for (see *Templates*).

All quilting, whether done by hand or by machine, should begin in the center of the quilt and move outward so that any shifting will be evenly distributed and will not detract from the finished quilt. Design areas can be outline-quilted and then filled in with more detail at your leisure. Filling in can be done in or out of the frame, since it will then be more stabilized.

HAND QUILTING

When hand quilting, I prefer the stab stitch with a #10 crewel needle. With practice, it produces the most perfect stitches on both the quilt top and the back of the quilt while leaving the quilt perfectly unruffled and unshifted, as is often the case with the running stitch. Strive for 9-12 quilting stitches per inch showing on the quilt top. I prefer quilting thread with a finish, such as JP Coats, since it is easier to thread into the needle, and it does not shred and knot-up as easily as uncoated threads. When quilting, put a knot into an 18" single thread and, from the top of the quilting surface, bury the knot in the batting about one inch from the first stitch. When ending the thread, bury the knotted end about an inch from the last stitch, again from the top of the quilting surface.

Quilting may be done in a large floor frame, a hanging frame, a standing hoop, a lap hoop, or without a frame altogether. Frames come in all sizes and shapes. The large floor frame offers the most stable control of the three layers of the quilt sandwich.

MACHINE QUILTING

Machine quilting has certainly entered the forefront of debate among quilting purists, especially as it relates to categories and awards in quilting competitions. Although I have not yet entered a machine quilted quilt in a major/international competition, when I feel that my machine quilting reflects some mastery, I will. Regardless of the collection of particular techniques included, a stunning quilt is a stunning quilt.

All quilted projects are not destined to become family heirlooms, nor do we have enough time to hand quilt every project we have designed or will design in the future. Clothing and children's quilts are particularly good candidates for machine quilting so as to withstand repeated washings. Similarly, "found" quilt tops and quilt tops which may not live up to our designed expectations are likely candidates for machine quilting.

Currently, I recommend four techniques with variations within each technique. The first, most basic technique includes straight line and in-the-seamline-ditch quilting, most commonly with a size #10-11 needle and regular sewing thread or fine clear nylon thread. The walking foot makes this very easy to do while preventing puckers on the backside. Without a walking foot, quilting lines should be limited to straight diagonals, enabling the quilter to stretch the project along the bias to reduce puckering. Presser foot pressure should be reduced to the minimum. With or without the walking foot, in-the-ditch stitching should be done on the "low" side of the seam (not the side where the seam allowances are) so as to avoid unsightly stitches or holes. A quilting bar is available for some sewing machine presser feet, as on the New Home. It screws onto the presser foot at the desired distance from the needle and sews evenly spaced rows of stitches with ease.

It is important to prevent any drag on the feeding of the quilt into the machine so the stitches will be consistent. After rolling both sides of a quilt in towards the center and securing these rolls with bicycle clips, throw the whole thing over a shoulder and feed it through the sewing machine on the dining room table. I maintain a normal sewing stitch length, except when quilting miniatures. Then I reduce the stitch length a bit. Aim to sew from the same raw edge of the quilt to the opposite raw edge. This will eliminate the time consuming and possibly structurally weakening task of tying-off and burying many threads and will avoid rippling between the quilted lines.

Although my own sewing machine requires no adjustments, other machines may require reducing the thread tension to "0" when using fine clear nylon thread through the needle. Almost all machines require loosening the bobbin tension screw for proper stitches to form on the backside of the quilt (loosen 90° at a time). Even top-of-the-line machines may require playing with the stitch length between 2.0 and 2.5 to produce puckerless, properly formed stitches on both the quilt top and back. If the thread tension cannot be reduced enough to avoid puckering on the quilt top, try placing the fine nylon thread on a cone holder or in a weighted liter soft drink bottle.

The bobbin thread should usually match the quilt top, with backing fabric matching the bobbin thread, also, except where special effects are intended. Since the emphasis is on the needle holes when machine quilting with nylon thread, it is usually undesirable to notice the bobbin thread peaking through to the quilt top here and there unless that is part of the design plan. A notable exception includes mimicking hand quilting. This is done by using a larger needle (such as a #14), a contrasting bobbin thread, and further loosening the bobbin tension screw to encourage the bobbin thread to show on the quilt top. Since clear nylon thread lies on the quilt top, the contrasting dots of bobbin thread appear to be hand quilted "stitches". If clear nylon thread must be used in the bobbin, it should be hand wound onto the bobbin. The nylon will stretch if it is machine wound. Also, the nylon may need to bypass the bobbin tension regulator altogether if the bobbin tension screw cannot be loosened enough. To prevent a stripped and useless bobbin screw, it may be wise to purchase a second bobbin case.

To follow a quilting design over a quilt surface no larger than 42" square, I use a clear zigzag foot which I have further cut out to produce as much visibility as possible. To be perfectly suitable for machine quilting, the quilting design should have a minimum number of starting and stopping points and no areas which must be sewn over more than once. Many quilting designs may be modified to accommodate, for example:

From this...

...to this.

Illus 5.

Since a 42" square or smaller quilt can be turned within the confines of the sewing machine, a regulated and consistent stitch results with the aid of the feed dogs. Holding the top thread, begin and end in the same hole, with all four threads being tied into two knots on the backside, trimmed off even, threaded into a #5 embroidery (large eye) needle, and buried in the batting. Do the same when the bobbin empties and then start again where you left off.

I prefer the fine, clear nylon thread because it prevents a thready appearance on the front of the quilt, but I use white thread on a white quilt top. The presser foot pressure should be at the minimum to allow smooth maneuvering around curves. If this remains difficult, frequent lifting of the presser foot will be necessary.

Large quilts *demand* free-motion quilting which allows maintaining the quilt in one basic position while moving the quilt forward, backward, and sideways under the moving needle. This technique requires a darning/embroidery foot with an arm which rests upon the screw holding the needle in place. This allows the presser foot to lift off of the quilt top each time the needle rises. The function of this foot is to release the quilt from the needle, in case it gets stuck as it rises. It also stabilizes the quilt, preventing it from vibrating to the point of being difficult to see where one is going. I like to cut out the front of my foot for added visibility; I do not want my visibility diminished by the plastic. Lower or cover the feed dogs.

Roll the sides of the quilt to the center, as directed above, and put the needle down in a spot where it will be easy to join up with later, such as a straight-ish portion of the quilting design (NOT a corner or a point). Strive to produce a consistent stitch length while following the quilt design. It takes some practice to keep from pushing the quilt top right off of the sewing machine table since your hands are all the control there is.

Again, hold the top thread as the first stitches are taken, and trim this thread flush with the quilt surface as soon as it can be done easily. As the starting point is approached, overlap the stitching ¼". Cut the first bobbin thread flush with the quilt back; pull the final top thread to the back, tie off with the final bobbin thread, and bury, as above. If you run out of thread and must start up where you left off, trim the last threads flush with the quilt

top and the quilt back, and begin sewing to overlap the last stitches by ¼". These two beginning threads will be tied off on the back side and buried, also.

With mastery of this technique (as consistent a stitch length as with feed dogs), starting and stopping will be the same as with the previous technique, and mixing the two techniques will look fine.

Although larger quilts *must* be quilted in a free-motion style, with practice it has become my favorite method with smaller projects, also. It is both the most versatile and the fastest technique of the three mentioned so far. The presser foot pressure remains at a minimum. A size #10-11 needle should be used, unless it has any trouble. Then use as small a needle as possible, just one size larger, to keep the holes as small as possible. Maintain a medium rate of speed. Too fast results in thready build-up; too slow results in uneven stitches and irregular lines. Develop a rhythm between the speed of the machine and the speed at which the quilt is moved. My thread choices are the same as for the technique with the zigzag foot above.

Stippling is the final machine quilting technique I use. It is a deceptively easy free-motion technique consisting of a very close meandering pattern in which a continuous line remains curvilinear, turning first away from and then back toward itself in a seemingly random pattern with lines maintaining a consistent ¹⁄₁₆"-⅛" distance from each other while never touching. With miniatures, to keep a proper perspective, these lines will almost touch. Avoid regular jigsaw shapes since any irregularity will become quite noticeable. The result is a heavily textured flat area which makes surrounding shapes appear to be stuffed. Set-up is the same as for free-motion machine quilting. Experiment with the results achieved from bobbin threads first matching and then contrasting with the quilt top. Stippling on clothing should be limited to little areas for accent since they will be too stiff to drape properly on the body. Larger stippling, more appropriately called "meandering," can be used effectively to fill in larger areas and backgrounds.

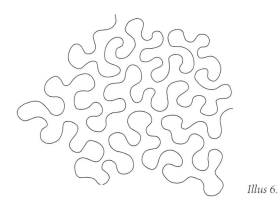

Illus 6.

As necessity is the mother of invention, I used a rather unorthodox technique to free-motion machine quilt the portraits onto *Plaids, Plaids, Plaids*. The many seam allowances, together with the dark plaids, made it impossible to see the details of the quilting design when placed onto the light table. I solved this problem by tracing the design onto a nonwoven sew-and-tear-away sheet which I then basted through the already-basted quilt sandwich. The tear-away product was pliable so it hugged the contours of the quilt and rolled up without being destroyed; it also did not tear with each stitch as tissue does when used in this manner. DO NOT tie off threads until after it has been removed so the knots will not be pulled out.

FINISHING

There are many ways to finish the edges of a quilt. The quilt top may be cut large enough to fold a border onto the back side. The quilt backing may be cut large enough to fold a border to the quilt top. The quilt top and the quilt backing may be cut the same size with ¼" turned to the inside and whipped into place. Piping may be stitched to the quilt top edge before these edges are whipped.

Binding may be sewn through all layers of the quilt's edges, turned to the back side (or front), and blindstitched into place. When I use binding, I prefer to cut it on the straight of grain to avoid puckering, unless I have a curved edge. In this case I cut the binding on the bias. My bindings are cut 2" wide in order to be folded in half before joining to the quilt top. This produces a folded edge to blindstitch into place along the ¼" seam taken to sew the binding onto the quilt. The 2" strips are joined with 45° diagonal seams to reduce bulk (seams are pressed open) with the resulting binding showing about ³⁄₁₆" on the front of the quilt.

Whether finishing with a border or with a binding, a decision must be made about the corners of each. Butted corners and mitered corners are the most frequently chosen. The choice should reflect more of the same found throughout the quilt top. For example, if an Amish quilt top employs butted corners on the internal borders, butted corners on the final border would be appropriate. However, if mitered corners or many diagonal seams have been used within a quilt top, mitered corners would be required.

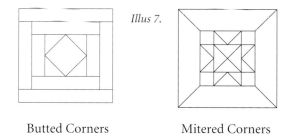

Illus 7.

Butted Corners   Mitered Corners

Mitering borders requires cutting all four borders the finished size of the quilt (plus twice the width of the border to be turned to the backside, if any) plus two seam allowances. To insure proper placement of the border onto the quilt top, the ends of the border should extend beyond the quilt top raw edge by the width of the finished border (plus the width of the finished turned border, if any). Sew from the intersection of the seam allowances in the corner of the quilt top to the same spot on the opposite end of the seam; do not sew from raw edge to raw edge. Threads may be tied, if desired, but do not trim them short if they are left untied.

When two borders have been joined to the quilt top and need to be mitered, place borders right sides together right on top of each other (quilt top will be folded on the diagonal from the corner). Draw a line on the wrong side of one of the borders from the point at which the corner stitch was taken to the outside corner of the border strip.

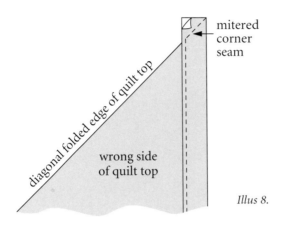

Illus 8.

Holding the quilt top out of the way, sew from the point where the last stitch hole was made at the corner of the quilt top to the outside corner along the drawn line. Tie off threads where the stitching started. Trim seam allowances to ¼", and press in the same direction as the seam allowances in the previous border's miter. For turning a border to the back side, fold it to the back after quilting. Then fold a miter into the corner on the back, turn under raw edges ¼", and blindstitch into place.

Mitering the binding again requires sewing to within ¼" of the quilt top's raw edge at the corner and tying off the threads. Next, fold the binding straight up, forming a 45° angle at the corner. Fold binding back down onto itself, with the fold even with the quilt top's raw edge. Sew from the folded edge to within ¼" of the quilt's next corner, and repeat all around the quilt. Join the ends of the binding with a 45° diagonal seam. Start sewing 6"

from the end of the binding strip in the middle of a side of the quilt. Trim batting and backing even with quilt top raw edges. Turn the binding to the back of the quilt and blind-stitch the folded edge and miters into place.

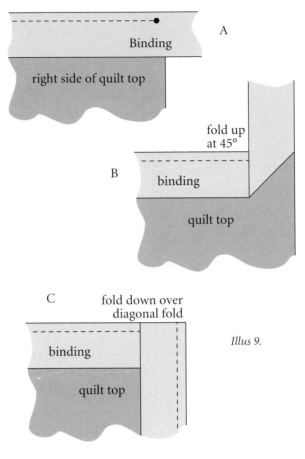

Illus 9.

A FINAL WORD

The foremost considerations with my own quilts are BALANCE, CONSISTENCY, and the UNEXPECTED. BALANCE includes color, texture, design elements, and quilting concentration. The UNEXPECTED can come from a touch of red or black in an otherwise light or soft quilt; emphasis on the background of a pattern block rather than the design portion; a mix of seemingly incompatible colors; placing the center of interest off-center; adding vining appliquéd flowers to a strongly geometric quilt; plaid fabrics with chintz; a print background rather than a solid neutral; or a portion of a pattern unit "falling" into the border. This can add something special which gives your quilt a spark of life all its own.

Style A Feathered Star

MATERIALS	9¼" STAR	18½"-20" STAR	37¼"-40" STAR	55½" STAR
Piecing time	5 hours	8 hours	9 hours	10 hours
SPEED GRIDS®, opt.	½"	1"	2"	3"
Background	½ yd light blue	½ yd black	1¼ yd chintz*	2¾ yd chintz*
"Feathers"	⅛ yd white ⅛ yd red solid	¼ yd pink solid	¼ yd small black print	½ yd small black print
Diamond tips	⅛ yd black	⅛ yd yellow	¼ yd black/pink print	¼ yd black/pink print
Star arms	⅛ yd dark blue print	⅛ yd floral print	⅜ yd floral print	⅜ yd floral print
Center triangles	⅛ yd blue/white check	⅛ yd pale pink solid	¼ yd dark rose solid	¼ yd dark rose solid
Center octagon	⅛ yd floral print	⅛ yd pink print ¼ yd turquoise scrap – dark print	12" square green print	½ yd green print
Surrounding triangles		½ yd each		
Binding			½ yd pink	1 yd pink
PATTERN TEMPLATES	T, U, (V), W, X, Y, Z	U1, V1, W1, X1, Y1, Z1	T2, U2, V2, W2, X2, Y2, Z2	T3, U3, V3, W3, X3, Y3, Z3
MARK FABRICS				
56 Triangle-blocks	½" SPEED GRIDS® or Z: red solid & white	1" SPEED GRIDS® or Z1: black & pink solid	2" SPEED GRIDS® or Z2: sm black print & chintz	3" SPEED GRIDS® or Z3: sm black print & chintz
16 Triangles	Z: white	Z1: black	Z2: chintz	Z3: chintz
8 Diamonds	Y: black	Y1: yellow	Y2: black/pink print	Y3: black/pink print
4 and 4-reverse	X: dark blue print	X1: floral print	X2: floral print	X3: floral print
8 Center Triangles	W: blue/white checked	W1: pale pink solid	W2: dark rose solid	W3: dark rose solid
1	T: floral print		T2: green print	T3: green print
8	U: light blue (or 4U and 4V)			
4		U1: black	U2: chintz	U3: chintz
4		V1: black	V2: chintz	V3: chintz
		Strips (see projects)	Strips (see projects)	

On page 15 is a chart listing yardage and templates for four feathered star projects. The **9¼" feathered star** pattern includes instructions and templates for a 14" square or circular miniature quilt with motifs suitable for machine quilting. Refer to Photo #1 for a variation which includes a quilted "sweater" covered with edge-to-edge 14" quilts. Only the center front star is pieced and appliquéd into place. For consistency, I surrounded my 9¼" star with eight background squares, although patterns are included for both background squares (U) and background triangles (V), so you may choose your own setting. (It is easier to turn under the edges of an unpieced background square or triangle than to turn under the pieced edges of the star itself.) Try the star on the *Birds-in-Air Jumper* bodice or the *Crazy Vest*, both found in this book.

The pattern for the **18½" feathered star** features a 9-patch floating in the center octagon as well as background strips surrounding each pattern block to produce 20" squares. Photo #2 illustrates five 18½" stars, each pieced in different color combinations and surrounded by large triangles before joining the other stars to produce a 74" quilt top. Turning a square pattern block "on point" in this fashion takes up more room with each pattern block while highlighting each block more. This quilt top has large areas that will accommodate plenty of feathery quilting motifs with or without the addition of some stuffed areas, or trapunto. Photo #1 illustrates one 18½" star in the center of a large *Style B Feathered Star*.

Add 1⅛" (finished) background strips to frame the **37¼" feathered star** if a 40" pattern block is preferred, see Photo #3. Although great alone as a wallhanging, a full size quilt could be created with five or nine stars.

Refer to Photo #3 also for the **55½" feathered star**. I particularly like to see larger stars (greater than about 25") framed with a border

of background fabric so they are more highlighted than when their tips touch the border and they appear to be boxed-in. I then frame this "self frame" with a contrasting 1½"-3" border and follow with a border wide enough (up to 15", solid or pieced) to cover the bed. Yardage for the 55½" star includes a solid, unpieced center octagon/square, but it would look great either pieced or appliquéd with a 15" (or 16") pattern block framed with ²⁷⁄₃₂" (or ¹¹⁄₃₂") finished strips to produce a 16¹¹⁄₁₆" finished square (needed to fit this star).

Since all of the *Style A Feathered Stars* have been treated a little differently in their presentation, further individualized instructions follow the general instructions.

ASSEMBLE STYLE A FEATHERED STARS

1. Piece all 56 triangle-blocks. Press seams toward "feathers." If not using SPEED GRIDS®, 56 triangles "Z" will need marking and cutting from each of the two colors forming the triangle-blocks. Further, if not using SPEED GRIDS®, trim seam allowances even, to avoid any shadow of dark fabric under lighter fabric (refer to the *Machine Piecing* section in *Winning Construction Tips*).

2. Piece six each Section A and Section B; two each Section C and Section D. Press all seams toward the top of the Section, trimming seam allowances even to avoid shadows.

3. Arrange Sections on a table like this to make remaining piecing easier:

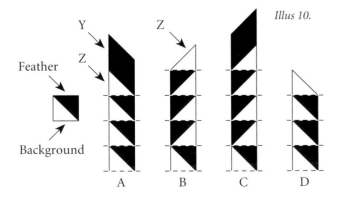

Illus 10.

4. Sew Section A to Section C. Sew to within ¼" of raw edge at spot marked with arrow. Press seam toward background.

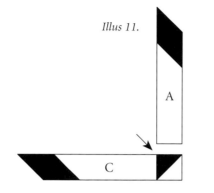

Illus 11.

5. Sew Section B to Star Arm X. Press seam toward X.

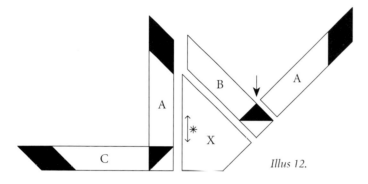

Illus 12.

6. Sew Section BX to Section AC. Press seam toward X.

7. Sew Section A to Section B. Sew to within ¼" at arrow. Press seam toward background.

8. Sew Triangle W to Star Arm X. Press seam toward X.

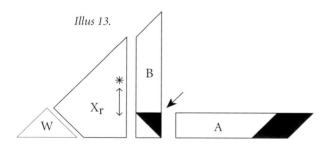

Illus 13.

9. Sew Section B to Section WX. Press seam toward X.

10. Sew portion illustrated in #8 to portion illustrated in #5. Press seam toward WX.

11. Sew Section A to Section B as illustrated in #8. Sew to within ¼" at arrow. Press seam toward background.

12. Repeat Steps 4 through 11 one time.

13. Sew Section B to Section D. Sew to within ¼" at arrow. Press seam toward background.

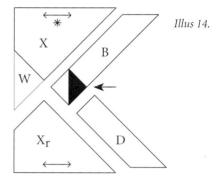

Illus 14.

14. Sew Star Arm X to Section BD. Press seam toward X.

15. Sew Triangle W to Star Arm X. Press seam toward X.

16. Sew Section WX to BDX. Press seam toward WX.

17. Repeat Steps 13 through 16 one time.

SEE INDIVIDUAL INSTRUCTIONS FOR 18½" FEATHERED STAR NOW.

18. Sew 4 Triangles W to the Center Octagon/Square T corners. Position Triangle W, right sides together, with raw edge along marked line closest to corner. Sew ¼" seam from W raw edge. (It should still look like perfect square.) Trim away T corner.

Align W edge with line on T

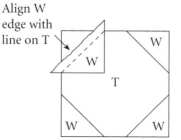

Illus 15.

17

19. Sew 2 sections illustrated in #13 to opposite sides of Center Octagon/Square T. Press seams toward XWX.

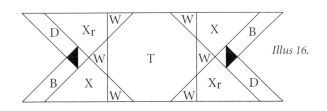

Illus 16.

20. Sew 3 strips of star together, as illustrated. Press seams toward center strip.

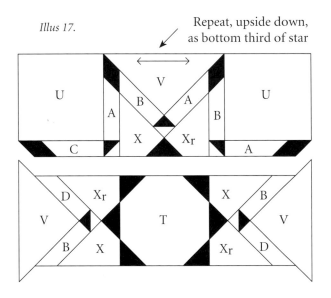

Illus 17.

Repeat, upside down, as bottom third of star

21. Sew 4 Squares U and 4 Triangles V (or 8 Squares U around 9¼" star) into place, pivoting at point ¼" from raw edge at corners where they join to AC and AB. Although sewing to the outside raw edges is desirable when joining most of the stars' U and V pieces, on the 9¼" star, sew all the way to the outside raw edge with the first seam joining U to the diamond tip, but only to the outside seam allowance with the other seam. This will make it easier to turn under the seam allowances for appliqué.

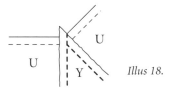

Illus 18.

14" Miniature Quilt with 9¼" Star

1. Appliqué feathered star to center of miniature quilt background fabric. Trim away background fabric behind feathered star to reduce bulk.

2. With 9¼" star centered, mark 14" square outline onto background fabric with water-soluble marker.

3. Using the feathered star miniature quilt portion on the next page, on a light table, trace quilting motifs around the pieced star with a water-soluble marker. Shaded areas may be stippled.

4. Machine or hand quilt.

5. See *Finishing* in *Winning Construction Tips*.

Quilted Sweater with 9¼" Star

Any sweatshirt pattern will do; simply make sure the quilted body will go over the head before adding ribbings. (Neckline ribbings are generally three-fourths the length of the neckline finished opening length.) Widen the ribbing to create a turtleneck, with or without crewneck ribbing, also.

1. Using the feathered star portion on the next page as a guide, draw a 9¼" pieced feathered star onto vellum or tracing paper.

2. Cut rough rectangles of body fabric 2" larger all around for each pattern piece of sweatshirt front, back, and sleeves. Repeat for backing and batting.

3. Mark 14" grid onto the rough rectangles of body top fabric with water-soluble marker, positioning star wherever you please.

4. On a light table, with the marker, trace feathered stars and quilting motifs in each 14" square.

Illus 19.

Machine quilting designs to surround 9¼" feathered star.

7/16"

5. Using the feathered star miniature quilt portion on page 19 again, trace quilting motifs around the stars, pieced or only drawn.

6. Baste top, batting, and backing together to quilt. Since so little piecing is in this "sweater", I chose to use "Cotton Classic" from Fairfield Processing rather than flannel for year-round wear since the flannel would have produced such a flat result with none of the desired relief from quilting.

7. After quilting, stitch around edges of each rectangle and put through 2-3 complete wash and dry cycles in the washing machine.

8. Cut out pattern pieces for "sweater" and sew together, trimming all seams to ¼" and finishing with a multi-stitch zigzag.

18½" or 20" Star

1. For center octagon/square in the star, with rotary cutter, cut one strip turquoise 1¹³⁄₁₆" wide across 26" of 45" yardage, one strip turquoise 1½" wide across 8" of yardage, one strip pink print 1½" wide across 8" of yardage, and one strip dark print 1½" wide across 2" of yardage. Although you may choose to cut one 1½" square (template S1) dark print, four 1½" squares pink print, and four 1½" squares turquoise for center 9-patch for only one 18½" star, instructions are given for cutting strips when more than one 9-patch is needed.

For speed piecing, further cut the one 1¹³⁄₁₆" turquoise strip into four 6⅛" pieces, the 1½" turquoise strip into two 4" pieces, and the 1½" pink print into one 4" and two 2" pieces.

Sew the 4" strip of pink print between two 4" strips of turquoise with ¼" seams. Press seams toward outer strips. Cut into two 1½" strips.

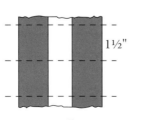

1½"

Illus 20.

Sew the 2" strip of dark print between two 2" strips of pink print, as above. Press seams toward center. Square up and trim to 1½".

Join these pieced strips into 3" (finished) 9-patch block (see piecing diagram). Press. Then sew 1¹³⁄₁₆" turquoise strips to each side of the block, mitering corners. Press. Represented as T in the star diagrams, the block should measure 6⅛" (5⅝" finished).

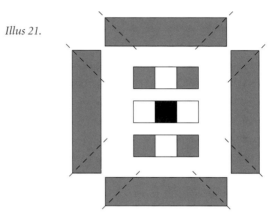

Illus 21.

Sew 4 Triangles W1 to corners of each 9-patch block using raw edge guides below, right sides together. Sew ¼" seam from raw edge. Trim away corners underneath.

Return to Step #19 and #20 in *Assemble Style A Feathered Stars*.

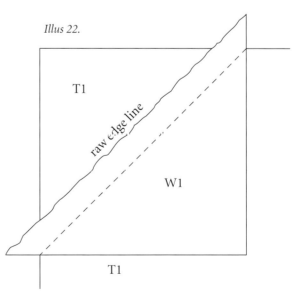

Illus 22.

T1

raw edge line

W1

T1

2. For 74" square quilt top (see Photo #2), the diagonal of the large triangles is sewn to each side of an 18½" feathered star block. For the large triangle template, draw a 13.08" right triangle (see ruler guide in *Pattern Template* section) with an 18½" diagonal, and add ¼" seam allowances all around. (See *Templates* in the *Winning Construction Tips* section.) The grainline should be parallel to one of the 13.08" sides.

3. For **20" feathered star**, cut four background strips 1¼" wide and 20½" long. Join to 18½" feathered star block, mitering corners.

37¼" or 40" Star

*Beginners should use a solid cream or small overall print as a background rather than a large print like this chintz. Large prints take lots of planning to avoid looking too cut up.

1. Some templates too large to include in this book need to be drawn (see *Templates* in *Winning Construction Tips* section):

Center octagon/square, T2, should be 11¹³⁄₁₆" square. Position template W2 in corners of T2, and mark diagonal on T2. Then, mark a line ½" toward corners from this diagonal line.

Background corner square U2 should be 11⁷⁄₁₆" square.

Background right triangle V2 should be drawn as a 10¹⁵⁄₁₆" right triangle with a 15⅜" diagonal. Then add ¼" seam allowances all around. Grainline should be along the diagonal.

2. I machine quilted a feathered wreath in the open areas surrounding the star for contrast against the sharp geometric lines of the star itself. Other rounded or flowing quilting motifs would be just as appropriate, as would vining appliqués.

3. For **40" feathered star**, cut four background strips 1⅜" wide and 40½" long. Join to 37¼" feathered star block, mitering corners.

55½" Star

*See note on chintz under 37¼" Star, above.

1. Some templates too large to include in this book need to be drawn (see *Templates* in *Winning Construction Tips* section):

Center octagon/square T3 should be 17³⁄₁₆" square. Position template W3 in corners of T3, and mark diagonal on T3. Then, mark a line ½" toward corners from this diagonal line.

Background corner square U3 should be 16¾" square. Background right triangle V3 should be drawn with 16¼" sides and a 22.97" diagonal (see ruler guide in *Pattern Template* section). Then add ¼" seam allowances all around. Grainline should be along the diagonal.

2. See #2 in individual instructions for 37¼" star, above.

Style B Feathered Stars

MATERIALS	25½"–30" STAR	51¾" STAR
Piecing time	9 hours	10 hours
SPEED GRIDS®, optional	1"	2"
Background	1½ yd black	2¾ yd black
"Feathers"	¼ yd turquoise	½ yd turquoise
Diamond tips	¼ yd turquoise	¼ yd turquoise
Star arms	¼ yd turquoise	¾ yd turquoise
1-piece Center square OR Center square background Center square contrast	⅜ yd OR ⅜ yd turquoise ¼ yd orange	⅝ yd OR ¾ yd turquoise ⅜ yd orange
PATTERN TEMPLATES	T4, U4, V4, X4, Y4, Z1	Y5, Z2 T5, U5, V5, X5, described in instructions
MARK FABRICS		
88 Triangle-blocks	1" SPEED GRIDS® or Z1: turquoise & black	2" SPEED GRIDS® or Z2: turquoise & black
16 Triangles	Z1: black	Z2: black
8 Diamonds	Y4: turquoise	Y5: turquoise
4 and 4-reverse	X4: turquoise	X5: turquoise
4	U4: black	U5: black
4	V4: black	V5: black
1-piece Center square	T4 OR pieced center described in instructions	T5 OR pieced center described in instructions

On the previous page is a chart listing yardage and templates for two feathered stars (refer to Photo #4 and Photo #1). Although I limited my color choices on this star, I have divided the yardage by pattern pieces in the chart so you may make your own choices. The **25½" star**, turned "on point" and surrounded by 18" right triangles, will produce a 36" (finished) square. See individual instructions for changing the orientation of both the center square and the star itself. The stars may be further enhanced with appliqué or pieced blocks in the center square. I particularly like to see stars this size framed with a border of background fabric so they are more highlighted than when their tips touch the border and they appear to be boxed-in. I then frame this "self frame" with a contrasting 1½"-3" border and follow with a border wide enough (up to 15", solid or pieced) to cover the bed. Another option would be to stand the star block "on point" to cover a larger area (see *Templates* in *Winning Construction Tips* section).

ASSEMBLE STYLE B FEATHERED STARS

1. Piece all 88 triangle-blocks. Press seams toward "feathers". If not using SPEED GRIDS®, 88 template Z will need marking and cutting from each of the two colors forming the triangle-blocks. Further, if not using SPEED GRIDS®, trim seam allowances even, to avoid any shadows of dark fabric under lighter fabric (refer to the *Machine Piecing* section in *Winning Construction Tips*).

2. Piece 4 each of Sections A, B, C, and D. Press seams toward top of the Section, trimming seam allowances to avoid shadows.

3. Arrange Sections on a table as shown at the top of the next column to make remaining piecing easier:

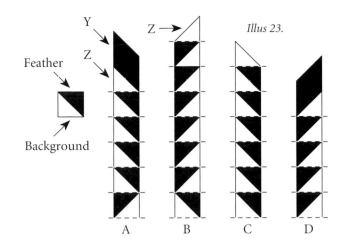

Illus 23.

4. Sew Section B to Star Arm X. Press seam toward X. Repeat with remaining Sections B.

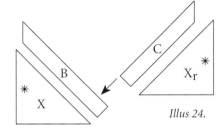

Illus 24.

5. Add Section C to all four of the above (leaving seam allowances free at arrow, to set-in large background square U later). Press seam toward background.

6. Sew Star Arm X-reverse to all 4 of the above, at Section C (see above). Press seam toward X. Set all four aside.

7. Sew Section D to black background triangle V. Press seam toward V. Repeat with remaining Sections D.

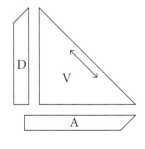

8. Add Section A to all 4 of the above. Press seam toward V.

9. Sew four large background squares U between Sections B and C, pivoting at point ¼" from raw edges at corner where B and C meet. Press seams toward U.

10. Appliqué center block with pattern of your choice, if you prefer, being mindful of the final orientation of the star. To finish stars, see individual instructions.

25½" or 30" Star

1. Piece an 8" (or 9") finished pattern block of your choice in the center square of the **25½" star** and frame it with $^{15}\!/_{16}$" (or $^{7}\!/_{16}$") finished strips. Or piece the *Star and Cross* pattern block, as seen in Photo #4. For speed, with a rotary cutter, cut one each 1½" wide turquoise and orange strips across 45" yardage for 9" (finished) block. Further cut the orange strip into eight 2½" pieces and four 1½" squares. Further cut the turquoise strip into four 3½" pieces and five 1½" squares. Cut one 3½" wide turquoise strip, then cut it into four 3½" squares. Cut two $^{15}\!/_{16}$" wide turquoise strips, then cut them into four 10⅜" pieces. Piece 8 turquoise and orange 1" (finished) triangle-blocks with 1" SPEED GRIDS® or with template Z1.

If you prefer templates to rotary cutting, you may use templates S1, S3, Z1, R2, and R4. Refer to piecing diagram below.

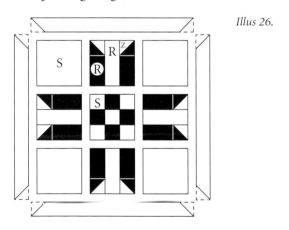

Illus 26.

2. Using the feathered star piecing diagram below as a guide, join portions of the feathered star into three horizontal rows. Press seams toward X.

3. Sew the three rows of the star together. Press seams toward center row.

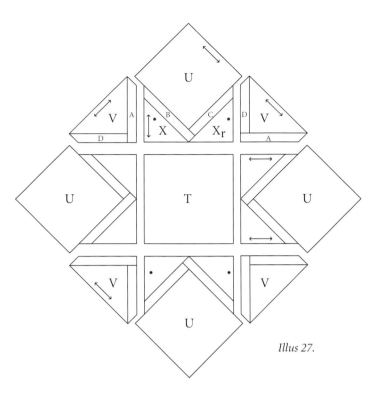

Illus 27.

4. For **30" feathered star**, cut four 1⅞" wide strips background fabric trimmed to 30½" lengths to frame 25½" star with mitered corners, if desired.

5. To change the orientation of the star and center block, switch the large background squares with the large background triangles, and vice versa. But to do so requires drawing a $6^{29}\!/_{32}$" square template to replace V4 and and an $8\!/_{16}$" right triangle (plus ¼" seam allowances all around) template to replace U4.

6. To stand the feathered star square "on point" (as it appears in the diagram above), draw an 18" right triangle template with 25½" diagonal, then add ¼" seam allowances all around (see *Templates* in *Winning Construction Tips* section). Grainline should be parallel to an 18" side. Join diagonal to each side of the feathered star block. This will also change the orientation of the center square.

7. Quilting designs which would contrast against the sharp geometric lines of the star would prove most appealing; such as, feathered wreaths, plumes, and vining motifs.

51¾" Star

1. Some templates too large to include in this book need to be drawn (refer to *Templates* in *Winning Construction Tips* section):

Center square T5, if not pieced, should be 20⅛" square.

Background corner square U5 should be 17⁵⁄₁₆" square.

Background right triangle V5 should be drawn with 12¹³⁄₁₆" sides and 18⅛" diagonal; then add ¼" seam allowances all around. Grainline should be along the diagonal.

Star Arm X5 right triangle should be drawn as illustrated, marking the longer side with an asterisk (both on the template and on the fabric); then add ¼" seam allowances all around.

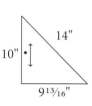

Illus 28.

2. Piece a 16" (or 18") finished pattern block of your choice in the center square of the 51¾" **star**, and frame it with 1⅜" (or ¹³⁄₁₆") finished strips, or piece the *Star and Cross* pattern block, as seen in Photo #4 and diagrammed above with 25½" star. For speed, with rotary cutter, cut two 2½" wide orange and one 2½" wide turquoise strips across 45" yardage for 18" pattern block. Further cut orange strips into eight 4½" pieces and four 2½" squares. Further cut turquoise strip into four 6½" pieces and five 2½" squares. Cut one 6½" wide turquoise strip, then cut it into four 6½" squares. Cut two (or four, if do not have 41" of usable yardage) 1⁵⁄₁₆" wide turquoise strips, then cut them into four 20⅛" pieces. Piece eight turquoise and orange 2" (finished) triangle-blocks with 2" SPEED GRIDS® or template Z2. You may use templates S2, S6, Z2, R7, and R10, if you prefer.

3. Using the feathered star piecing diagram above with the 25½" feathered star as a guide, join portions of the star into three horizontal rows. Press seams toward X.

4. Sew the three rows of the star together. Press seams toward center row.

5. To change the orientation of the star and center block, switch the large background squares with the large background triangles, and vice versa. But to do so requires drawing a 13⁵⁄₁₆" square template to replace V5 and a 16¹³⁄₁₆" right triangle (plus ¼" seam allowances all around) template to replace U5. (See *Templates* in *Winning Construction Tips*.)

6. To stand the feathered star square "on point" (as it appears in the piecing diagram), draw a 36⁵⁄₁₆" right triangle template with a 51¾" diagonal, then add ¼" seam allowances all around. Grainline should be parallel to a 36⁵⁄₁₆" side. Join the diagonal to each side of the feathered star block. This will also change the orientation of the center square.

7. For quilting ideas, see #7 under *25½" STAR*.

Clamshell Medallion

60½" square

MATERIALS

Scraps or ⅛ yd each, 26 different fabrics with equal distribution lights, mediums, and darks

2½ yd wine print, if heavily quilted OR 3⅛ yd, if mitered corners and quilted ray lines

Scraps or ⅛ yd each, 3 complimentary fabrics for log cabin corners

2¾ yd black

3¾ yd backing

80-20 batting, plus some loose fiberfill

PATTERN TEMPLATES

Make templates for clamshell and log cabin corner strips (or use rotary cutter for log cabin strips. (Refer to *Templates* in *Winning Construction Tips* section).

CENTER CLAMSHELL MEDALLION

1. Cut out 4 clamshells from each of 24 fabrics and 2 clamshells from each of 2 fabrics (for the four clamshells in the center). I used 2 black and 2 medium-blue print clamshells.

2. Join the 2 black center clamshells by sewing together the pointed tips. Sew tips of one medium-blue print and one blue-on-white print clamshell, then join to black clamshells. Repeat with "twin" set at opposite side of black clamshell pair. To piece curves easily, pin and sew from center of curve to outer edge; return to center to pin and sew other half.

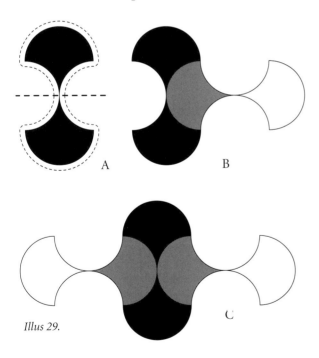

Illus 29.

3. Continue building with pairs of clamshells, from the center outward, referring to photo of quilt, until central medallion measures 10 clamshells along each of four sides.

4. Press 28½" black square in half both lengthwise and widthwise to find the center. With right side of fabric facing up, center clamshell medallion "square" onto black square. Pin in place. Turn under ¼" seam allowances all along clamshell edges, and blindstitch into place.

5. Carefully cut away black fabric from behind pieced clamshell so only one layer of fabric remains.

LOG CABIN CORNERS

1. Cut 4 strips from each pattern template (or with rotary cutter, noting finished dimensions on templates).

2. Begin with the pink triangles, and join one strip at a time to it, beginning with the 4¼" brown strip. Press after each addition.

3. Center log cabin corners along each side of the 28½" black appliqued square, and sew into place with ¼" seams.

ASSEMBLE QUILT

1. If planning to quilt rays from the center, as in photo, cut four wine print borders 12½" x 53", and sew, mitering corners. Press.

If planning other quilted designs, cut two wine print borders 12½" x 29" and two borders 12½" x 53". Join by butting shorter borders into longer borders. Press.

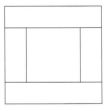

Illus 30.

2. Fold each border in half to find lines on which points of 28½" black square will lay.

3. Lay clamshell medallion with log cabin corners on top of wine print "frame". Secure with pins. Turn under raw edges of black square and log cabin corners ¼", and blindstitch into place. Press.

26

4. Cut away any wine print underneath black square or log cabin corners leaving a single layer of fabric overall.

5. Cut four black borders 5½" x 63". Join to wine print borders, mitering corners. Press. 1¼" will be turned to the backside of the quilt after quilting.

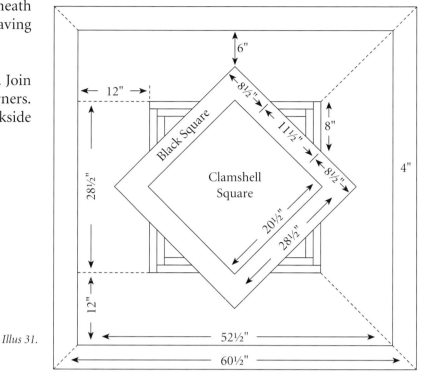

Illus 31.

QUILT AND FINISH

1. To piece backing, refer to *Quilting* in *Winning Construction Tips* section.

2. Before sandwiching the three layers of the quilt together, set a tuft of fiberfill on the wrong side of each clamshell. This will give additional "puff" to each shell. This will also necessitate basting the layers of the quilt together with the top face down.

3. Quilt "in-the-ditch" around each clamshell and between each "log" in the log cabin corners, plus the outer edge of those corners. With yard/meterstick and drafting tape, mark rays of quilting lines from center of quilt top, avoiding clamshells and log cabin corners,

evenly distributing between lines drawn in an "X" between the four corners of the quilt and between an "X" drawn horizontally and vertically through the points of the black square. Or quilt a ¾" grid, marked with drafting tape, in the wine print to really make the clamshell medallion and log cabin corners stand out. Quilt in-the-ditch between wine print and black border. Consider quilting clamshells in the black border.

4. After quilting through 4" of the black border, trim batting and backing even with that line (press or mark with fabric marker). Turn black to backside, mitering corners. Turn under ¼" seam allowance, and blindstitch into place.

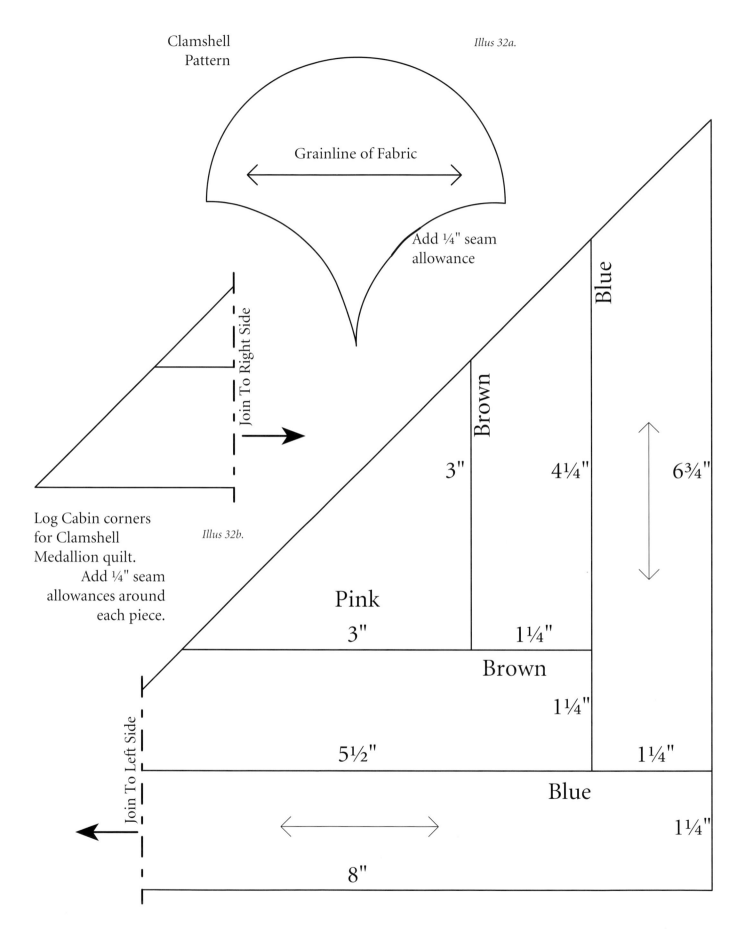

Clamshell
Pattern

Illus 32a.

Grainline of Fabric

Add ¼" seam
allowance

Join To Right Side

Log Cabin corners
for Clamshell
Medallion quilt.
Add ¼" seam
allowances around
each piece.

Illus 32b.

Blue

Brown

3"

4¼"

6¾"

Pink

3"

1¼"

Brown

1¼"

Join To Left Side

5½"

1¼"

Blue

1¼"

8"

28

Birds-In-Air-Jumper

Sizes: Small = 6-8

Medium = 10-12

Large = 14

Extra Large = 16

Directions are given for size SMALL with sizes MEDIUM, LARGE, and EXTRA LARGE in parentheses, below.

MATERIALS

1" SPEED GRIDS® (Speed-piece and machine quilt this bodice in 18 hrs!) Or use template Z1, if you prefer.

3½ yds light blue solid (I used oxford cloth)

¼ yd each, 3 plaids (appears to be 7)

1½ yds black piping

4⅞ yds black bias tape, double-fold (may make own)

6 pant hooks, OR eight ⅝" buttons

1 yd muslin for bodice backing

2 snaps

Tissue, vellum, or newsprint

Water-soluble marker

PATTERN PIECES

1. ¼" seam allowances included in pieced pattern blocks. ⅝" seam allowances included in clothing construction.

2. Carefully remove *FRONT* and *BACK BODICE* pattern pages from book, tracing one side of each page onto vellum. Trace appropriate size *FRONT* and *BACK BODICE* pieces onto folded tissue, vellum, or newsprint. Cut out.

3. To draw skirt pattern piece, refer to diagram above. Tape together two large pieces of tissue or newsprint 42" (42½"-43"-43") x 29" (31"-34"-35"). Fold in half so first measurement remains intact along center fold and the corners of resulting rectangle are 90°. (To shorten skirt, take it out at a line drawn horizontally, ⅓ of the way down from the top.)

To find point "A", measure down from "top" edge along center fold ⁷⁄₁₆".

To find point "B", measure up left side of rectangle 13" (14"-15½"-16").

To find point "C", measure from upper right corner ¾".

Draw straight line between "B" and "C" for skirt side.

Gently curve lines "AB"and "CD" to avoid any "V" at center fold. Cut out.

Mark an "X" three inches down on side seam.

Illus 33.

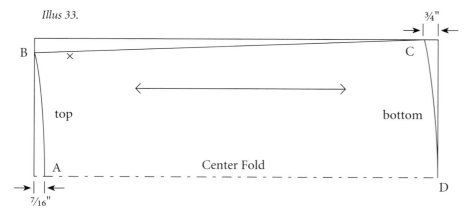

29

PATTERN BLOCK CONFIGURATION

(Each square = one pattern block. Notice split blocks, which can reduce number of required pattern blocks to piece.)

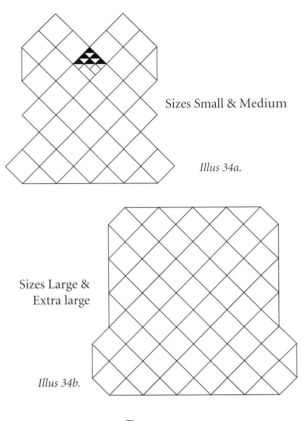

Sizes Small & Medium

Illus 34a.

Sizes Large &
Extra large

Illus 34b.

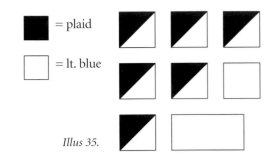

= plaid

= lt. blue

Illus 35.

Birds-In-Air pattern block piecing diagram.

BODICE

1. For sizes SMALL and MEDIUM, with plaids and light blue solid, piece 228 - 1" triangle-blocks with 1" SPEED GRIDS® or template Z1. (Takes 4 hrs with SPEED GRIDS®!) For sizes LARGE and EXTRA LARGE, piece 396 (in 6½ hrs with SPEED GRIDS®).

2. Categorize triangle-blocks into piles of similar appearance. There may be as many as twelve categories.

3. For sizes SMALL and MEDIUM, with rotary cutter and light blue solid cut 38 -1½" squares (or use template S1) and 38 -1½" x 2½" rectangles (or use template R2). For sizes LARGE and EXTRA LARGE, cut 66 -1½" squares and 66 -1½" x 2½" rectangles.

4. Refer to pattern block diagram to piece 38 pattern blocks for sizes SMALL and MEDIUM and 66 pattern blocks (or less, see configurations, left) for sizes LARGE and EXTRA LARGE. Sew pieces together into rows, then sew rows into pattern blocks. Press all seams in alternating rows in alternating directions for ease in perfectly matching seamlines and for reducing bulk. Since the pattern block has an uneven number of rows, press half of the top rows to one direction and half to the other. This also insures even distribution of seam allowances which, in pattern blocks with such small pieces, provides a substitute for batting.

Evenly distribute triangle-blocks from piles for balanced appearance across bodice.

5. Refer to *Pattern Block Configurations* to join pattern blocks for FRONT BODICE. Sew blocks together into diagonal rows, then sew rows into configuration needed. Fewer blocks may be needed if some of the blocks are cut in half on the diagonal, especially for size LARGE. Lay FRONT BODICE pattern on top of pieced pattern blocks as they are joined into the LARGE configuration.

6. Using FRONT BODICE pattern as a guide, cut out muslin rough rectangle, 2" larger all around. Pin, wrong sides together, to FRONT BODICE Pattern Block Configuration in preparation to quilt.

7. With light blue threads, machine quilt in-the-ditch along all horizontal and vertical pieced lines and in one diagonal direction, extending quilting lines across unpieced light blue areas in each pattern block.

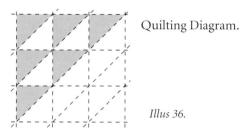

Quilting Diagram.

Illus 36.

8. Sew around outer edges. Wash in warm water, and dry.

9. Lay FRONT BODICE pattern piece on top of quilted fabric, and cut out.

10. Wrong sides together, pin BACK BODICE lining to *BACK BODICE* of light blue, wrong sides together.

11. Sew eight buttonholes, as marked, if desired, on FRONT and BACK BODICE at waist and shoulders. Or, see *FINISHING JUMPER #2*, below.

12. Trim all bodice edges except waistline to a ¼" seam allowance (trim away ⅜").

13. Encase shoulder, then neck and armhole, then side raw edges with black double-fold bias tape on both FRONT and BACK BODICE.

14. On ⅝" seamline, baste black piping to FRONT and BACK BODICE at waist, turning ends to inside.

PREPARE SKIRT PANELS

1. Cut out two skirt panels and 2 and 2-reverse pockets.

2. On right side of two skirt panels, mark five foldlines 3" apart beginning 5¼" up from bottom edge with water-soluble marker.

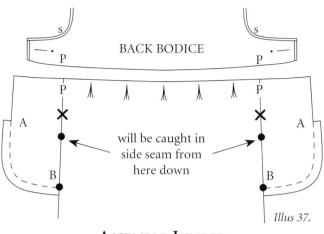

Illus 37.

ASSEMBLE JUMPER

1. Finish unnotched edge on four pockets above ⅝" seam allowance portion.

2. Sew two pockets to BACK SKIRT, matching "X's". Sew from top edge down to dot marked on pocket below "X". Clip from raw edges to within ¼" of dot. Press seam toward BACK SKIRT. Trim this portion of the seam to ¼" and finish edges.

3. Gather BACK SKIRT top edge. Line up "P's" on BODICE BACK and POCKET-SKIRT seam, see diagram above. Right sides together, sew SKIRT to BACK BODICE. Press seam allowances up toward BACK BODICE. Trim seam allowances close to stitching.

4. Cover waistline seam allowances on inside with bias tape, opened out and whipped into place.

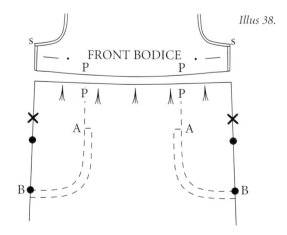

Illus 38.

5. Sew two pockets to FRONT SKIRT, matching "X's". Sew from top edge down to dot. Clip from raw edges to within ⅛" of dot. Trim seams to ¼".

6. Fold pockets to inside along seamline.

7. Gather FRONT SKIRT top edge. Line up "P" on FRONT BODICE with POCKET raw/finished edge. Allow minimal gathering first couple of inches in from sides for a more slenderizing look. Right sides together, sew FRONT BODICE to SKIRT. Trim seam allowances close to stitching.

8. Cover waistline seam allowances on inside, as in #4 above.

9. Sew FRONT BODICE and BACK POCKET together between "A" and "B". Sew again, ⅛" - ¼" into seam allowance. Trim.

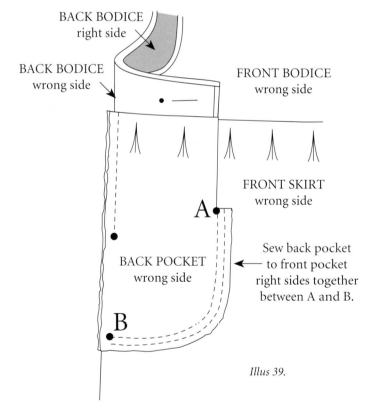

Illus 39.

10. Sew side seams: With jumper wrong side out, tuck fold of FRONT POCKET and FRONT SKIRT side seam portion below dot in between BACK POCKET and BACK SKIRT side seam, with all four raw edges even. This is much easier to understand by looking at diagram at bottom of left column.

If you were looking *through* this diagram with X-ray vision, you would see, in this order,

    a. wrong side BACK POCKET on top

    b. right side FRONT POCKET

    c. wrong side FRONT SKIRT

    d. right side BACK SKIRT

Sew through all four layers from dot to bottom edge of SKIRT. Clip seam allowances to within ¼" below "B".

11. Edgestitch ¹⁄₁₆" from edge of FRONT POCKET/SKIRT side seam folded edge.

12. Press side seams open below pockets. Fold SKIRT, wrong sides together, along five marked foldlines, and sew ¾" tucks. Press tucks down.

FINISHING JUMPER

1. Turn up hem 4" to hide hem stitching under bottom tuck.

2. If buttons and buttonholes were not made, align pant hooks with button and buttonhole markings on FRONT and BACK BODICE at waist and at one shoulder. Tack other shoulder into place permanently, if desired. Or, sew buttons at dots marked on inside of FRONT BODICE and on outside of BACK BODICE.

3. Sew snaps at "S", as illustrated, for more slenderizing appearance.

HANDBAG in photo on page 38 illustrates how special a handbag can look with even a tiny pieced and quilted inset (in this case, roughly 5"x 7").

Style A Feathered Star

9¼", shown on garment

Background Quilt: Variation on Style B 51¾" Feathered Star
with 18½" Style A Feathered Star in center.
Made by Margie Wedel.

Style A Feathered Stars

18½" each

Style A Feathered Star

37¼"

Style B Feathered Stars

51¾"

Draped variations, from left to right, by Bird Sherry, Marijane Deen (tree skirt), and Carol Willson.

Clamshell Medallion

60" square

Birds-in-Air Jumper and Handbag

Denim Grape Basket, 5", modeled by Morgan Taylor Hester.

Plaid Love-Apple Tree

54" square

Canadian Geese in Straw Wreath

42" square

August Pecan and Redbud

40" x 52"

Pieced with the help of Debbie Maurer and Inell Partin.

Crazy Vest

Black Magnolia

84" square

Amish English Ivy

84" square

Grape Basket Miniature

17½" square

Black Magnolia Handbag

45

Christmas Ribbons

47¾" square

Plaids, Plaids, Plaids

39⅝" square

Chintz Ruffled Pillow

28" square without ruffles

Pieced and assembled by Ann Siegert.

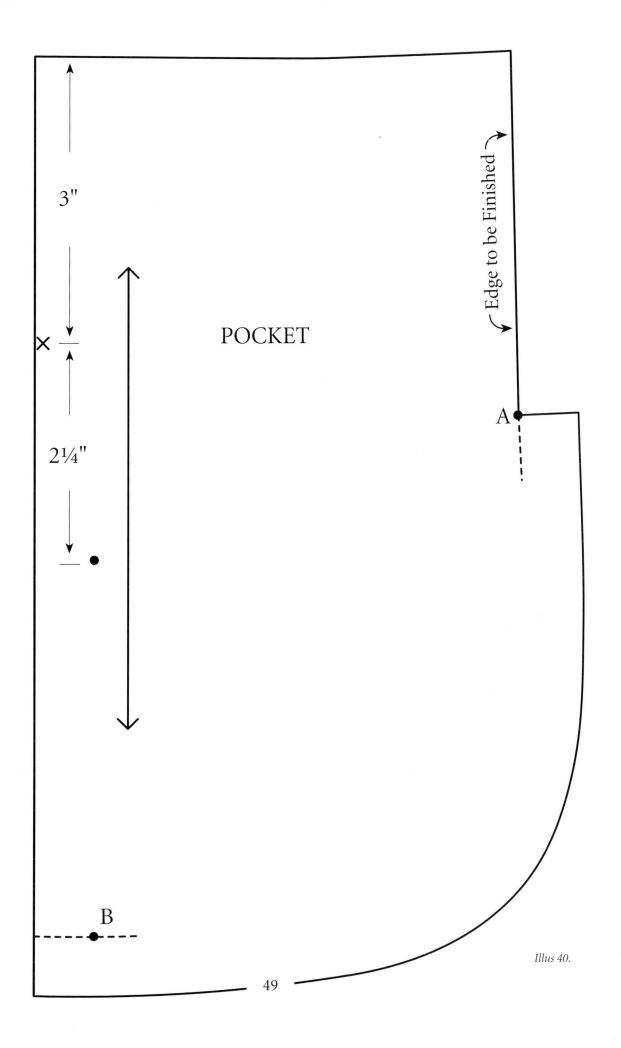

3"

POCKET

2¼"

×

Edge to be Finished

A

B

49

Illus 40.

Plaid Love-Apple Tree

Materials	2½" Tree	5" Tree	10" Tree	15" Tree
SPEED GRIDS®, opt	½"	1"	2"	3"
Plaid	⅛ yd	¼ yd	½ yd	1 yd
Black background & Appliqué	¼ yd	½ yd	1¼ yd	3 yd*
Light green triangles	⅛ yd	¼ yd	⅜ yd	½ yd
Dark green border	⅛ yd	¼ yd	¼ yd	½ yd
Magenta border	⅛ yd	¼ yd	½ yd	¾ yd
Orange	scrap	scrap	scrap	¼ yd
Turquoise appliqué				¼ yd
Pattern Templates	S , Z	S1, Z1	S2, Z2	S3, Z3
MARK FABRICS				
83 Triangle-blocks black and plaid	½" SPEED GRIDS® or Z	1" SPEED GRIDS® or Z1	2" SPEED GRIDS® or Z2	3" SPEED GRIDS® or Z3
1 Triangle-block black and orange	same	same	same	same
5 Squares black	S	S1	S2	S3
8 Triangles black	Z	Z1	Z2	Z3
1 Rectangle orange	¾" x 1½"	1" x 2"	1¼" x 5"	1½" x 8"

Above is a chart listing yardage and templates for four sizes of quilts based upon the ever popular *Pine Tree* pattern block; however, appliqué patterns are included for the **54"** quilt only. (The 54" quilt takes only 14 hours to piece with 3" SPEED GRIDS®!) As can be seen in the photo, plaids are very striking in this quilt. The **2½"** and **5"** pattern blocks are wonderful for clothing, handbags, box tops, and ornaments, and of course the 2½" block is a perfect choice for a miniature quilt. The **10"** block is perfect in a quilt alone or with other pattern blocks. If you prefer a tree block "on point" within a square for an original project, use the template measurements included for the light green triangles in photo #7.

54" Quilt

(15" Pine Tree)

1. For large light green triangle template, draw 11½" right triangle with 16¼" diagonal; add ¼" seam allowances all around. Grainline should be along one short side.

2. Refer to layout diagram below for black fabric in order to have enough fabric for bias appliqué strips when needed.

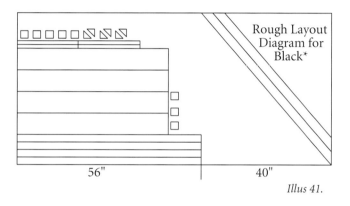

Rough Layout Diagram for Black*

56"   40"

Illus 41.

3. Piece all 88 plaid and black triangle-blocks and one orange and black triangle-block. It takes 1½ hours with 3" SPEED GRIDS®, or 6½ hours with template Z3! Press seams toward black.

4. With rotary cutter and black fabric, cut five 3½" squares and eight 3⅞" triangles. Template Z3 may be used, if preferred.

5. Lay out pieces for *Pine Tree* pattern block in order to balance colors in plaids over block. Refer to piecing diagram. Sew block together, first in rows, then into a square. Press each row before joining to next row, alternating direction of seam allowances in each successive row.

6. With wrong sides together, fold 1½" x 8" orange strip in half lengthwise. Sew ¼" seam and trim seam allowances close to stitching. Align seam down the middle of underside of strip. Place seam-down into place. Pin to hold.

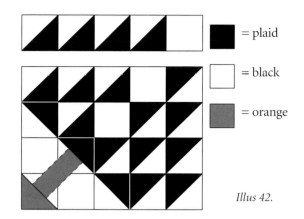

= plaid

= black

= orange

Illus 42.

With seam ripper, open seams to insert top and bottom edges of orange tube into seams in pattern block. Restitch seams. With orange thread, blindstitch into place.

7. With rotary cutter and black, cut four 1⅛" x 16¾" strips. Frame pattern block with these strips, mitering corners. Press.

8. Mark and cut four large light green triangles (with template made in #1 above). Join diagonal of triangles to sides of framed pattern block. Press.

9. With rotary cutter and dark green, cut four 3½" x 29½" strips. Join to light green square, mitering corners. Press.

10. With rotary cutter and magenta, cut four 5½" x 39½" strips. Join to dark green border, mitering corners. Press

11. With rotary cutter and black, cut four 5" x 48½" strips. Join to magenta border, mitering corners. Press.

12. For sawtooth border to have a balanced appearance, divide remaining plaid-and-black triangle-blocks into piles based upon dominant characteristics. Do not over-limit the number of piles; try to have two to four in each one, though. You might have 7-12 piles, for example. Distribute these piles somewhat equally into four piles for the four borders. Lay out one border at a time, distributing strong characteristics over the row for balance.

Include one black triangle at both ends of each border for mitered corners. Sew sawtooth borders to black border. Press.

13. For appliqué, using a light table, trace flowering vine appliqué and quilting motifs onto quilt top. (Trace motifs onto tracing paper first if they are too difficult to see.)

On right side of fabrics, trace appliqué flower pieces and leaves onto orange, turquoise, and black. Add ⅛"-¼" seam allowances "by eye" as cut out.

Cut 1" wide strips of black on the bias to produce an 80" strip when joined with 45° diagonal seams. Wrong sides together, sew ¼" seams. Trim seam allowances close to stitching. Align seam along underside of strip (a knitting needle is helpful), then center this tube over vining lines in two opposite corners of magenta border (refer to photo). With black thread, blindstitch into place.

Appliqué all leaves into place, including those on large flowers.

Appliqué flowers, following order as numbered on pattern pieces.

14. To quilt, I used cable quilting motifs on dark green and black borders. The light green large triangles were quilted by drawing a line between opposite corners of the green square, then using a bar screwed onto my sewing machine's presser foot to machine quilt evenly spaced lines from and including that line. ¼" drafting tape could be used, if hand-quilting.

Outline quilting was done in every seam, plus ¼" inside each triangle in the tree pattern block and in the sawtooth border, including the solid black squares in the tree pattern block to mimic the triangles, for consistency (diagram follows). The vining flower motifs in the magenta border were hand quilted with black thread.

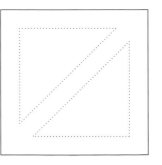

Illus 43.

15. To finish, with a rotary cutter, cut 2" wide strips of black on the straight of the grain to produce a length of 225" when joined with 45°diagonal seams. See *Finishing* in *Winning Construction Tips.*

36" Love-Apple Tree Quilt
(10" Pine Tree)

Follow directions given for 54" quilt, referring to charts and quilt diagram for particular requirements and dimensions for 36" quilt.

For light green triangle template, draw 7¾" right triangle with 11" diagonal; add ¼" seam allowances all around. Grainline should be along one short side.

With rotary cutter and black, cut five 2½" squares (2" finished) and eight 2⅞" triangles (2" finished), or template Z2 may be used, if you prefer.

Cut 1¼" x 6" orange strip; sew as in Step #6.

With rotary cutter and black, cut four 1" x 11½" strips to frame tree block.

With rotary cutter and dark green, cut four 2½" x 20" strips. Sew as in Step #9.

With rotary cutter and magenta, cut four 3¾" x 26½" strips. Sew as in Step #10.

With rotary cutter and black, cut four 3½" x 32½" strips. Sew as in Step #11.

Diagram of Quilt

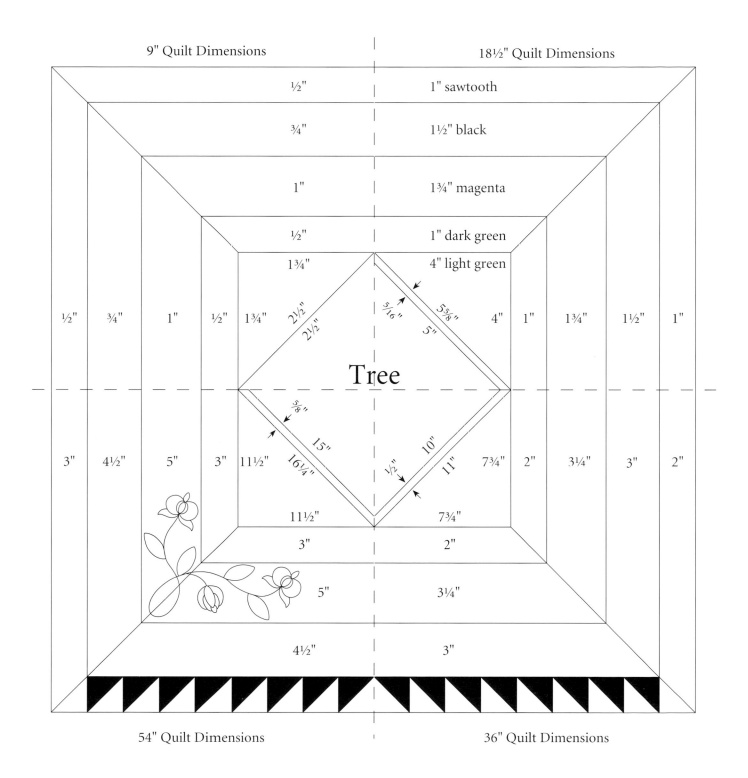

9" Quilt Dimensions   18½" Quilt Dimensions

½"   1" sawtooth

¾"   1½" black

1"   1¾" magenta

½"   1" dark green

1¾"   4" light green

½"   ¾"   1"   ½"   1¾"   2½"   2½"   5/16"   5 5/8"   5"   4"   1"   1¾"   1½"   1"

Tree

5/8"   15"   16¼"   ½"   10"   11"

3"   4½"   5"   3"   11½"   7¾"   2"   3¼"   3"   2"

11½"   7¾"

3"   2"

5"   3¼"

4½"   3"

54" Quilt Dimensions   36" Quilt Dimensions

Illus 44.

53

18½" Love-Apple Tree Quilt

(5" Pine Tree)

Follow directions given for 54" quilt, referring to charts and quilt diagram for particular requirements and dimensions for 18½" quilt.

For light green triangle template, draw 4" right triangle with 5⅝" diagonal; add ¼" seam allowances all around. Grainline should be along one short side.

With rotary cutter and black, cut five 1½" squares (1" finished) and eight 1⅞" triangles (1" finished), or template Z1 may be used.

Cut 1" x 3" orange strip; sew as in Step #6.

With rotary cutter and black, cut four $^{13}/_{16}$" x 6⅛" strips to frame tree block.

With rotary cutter and dark green, cut four 1½" x 10½" strips. Sew as in Step #9.

With rotary cutter and magenta, cut four 2¼" x 14" strips. Sew as in Step #10.

With rotary cutter and black, cut four 2" x 17" strips. Sew as in Step #11.

9" Love-Apple Tree Quilt

(2½" Pine Tree)

Follow directions given for 54" quilt, referring to charts and quilt diagram for particular requirements and dimensions for 9" quilt.

For light green triangle template, draw 1¾" right triangle with 2½" diagonal; add ¼" seam allowances all around. Grainline should be along one short side.

With rotary cutter and black fabric, cut five 1" squares (½" finished) and eight 1⅜" triangles (½" finished), or template Z may be used.

Cut ¾" x 2" orange strip; sew as in Step #6.

With rotary cutter and dark green, cut four 1" x 4½" strips. Sew as in Step #9.

With rotary cutter and magenta, cut four 1½" x 6½" strips. Sew as in Step #10.

With rotary cutter and black, cut four 1¼" x 8" strips. Sew as in Step #11.

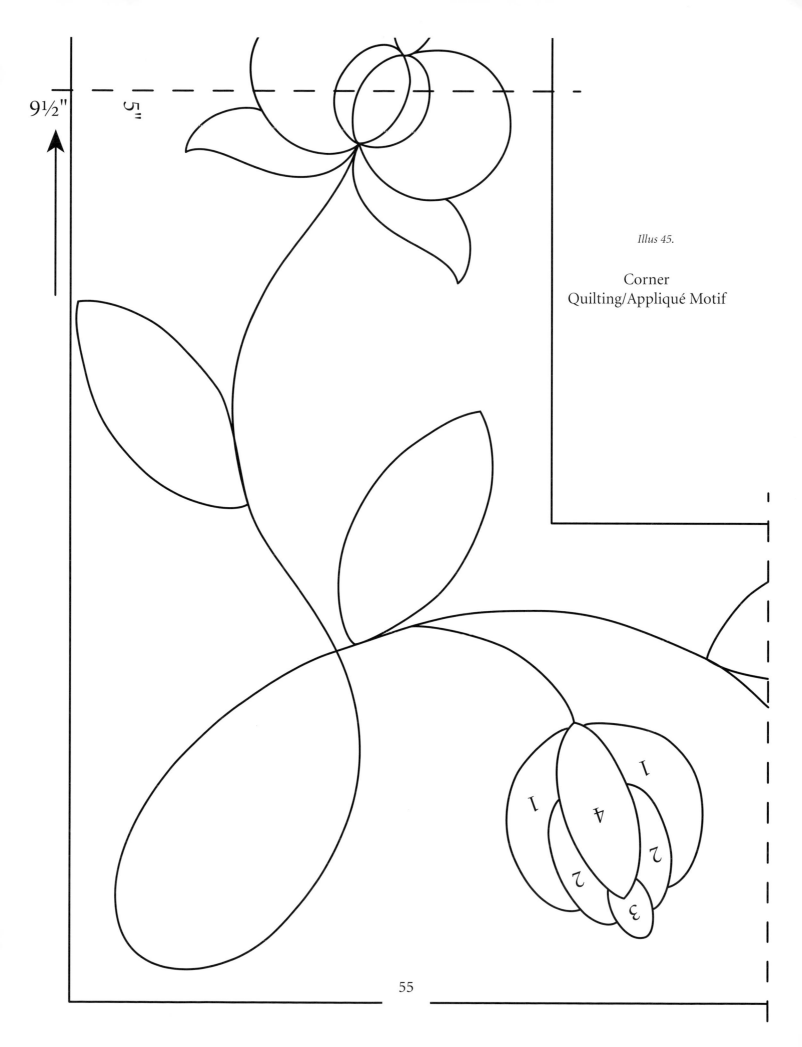

9½"

5"

Illus 45.

Corner
Quilting/Appliqué Motif

Extension of corner quilting/appliqué motif.

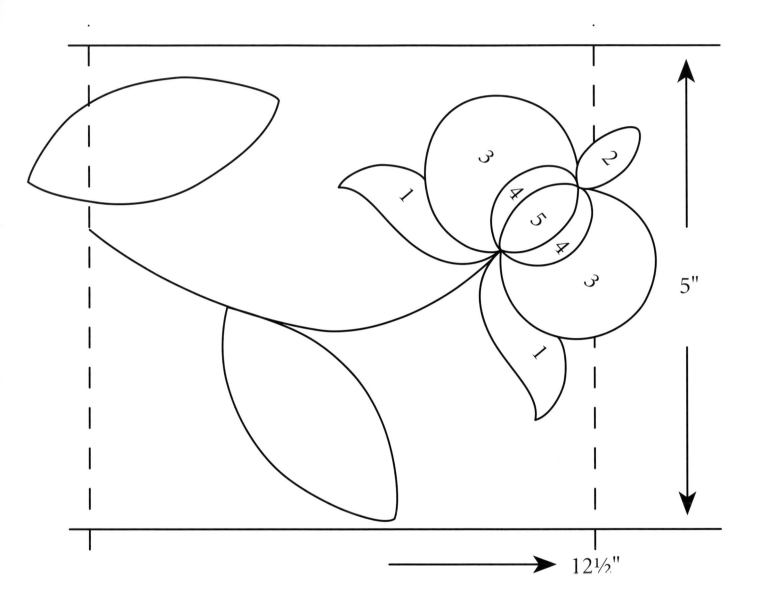

5"

12½"

Illus 47.

5"

Left half of quilting motif between corner motifs

Join to right half

5"

Join to left half

Right half of quilting motif between corner motifs

5"

Illus 48.

58

Corner
Quilting
Motifs

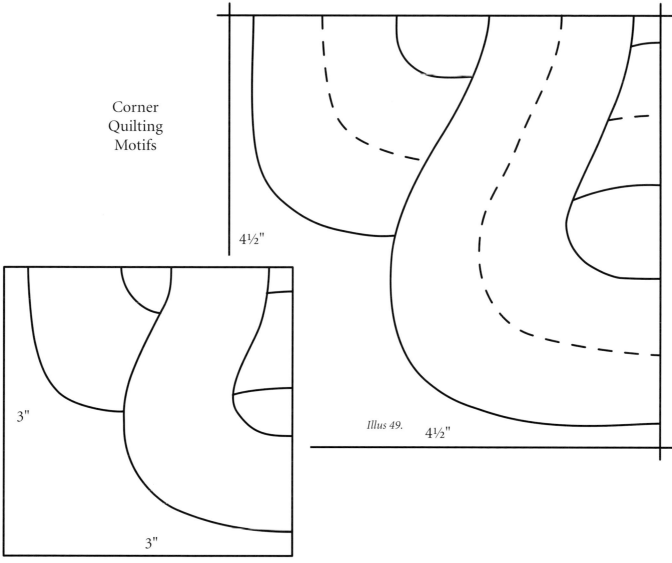

4½"

4½"

Illus 49.

3"

3"

Illus 50.

Illus 51.

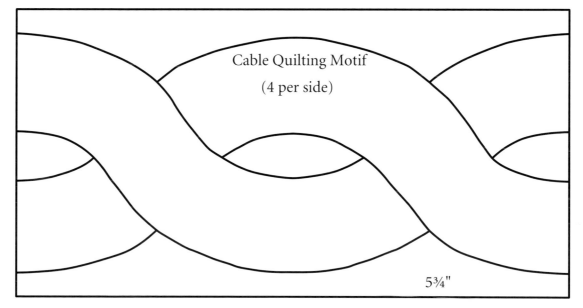

Cable Quilting Motif

(4 per side)

5¾"

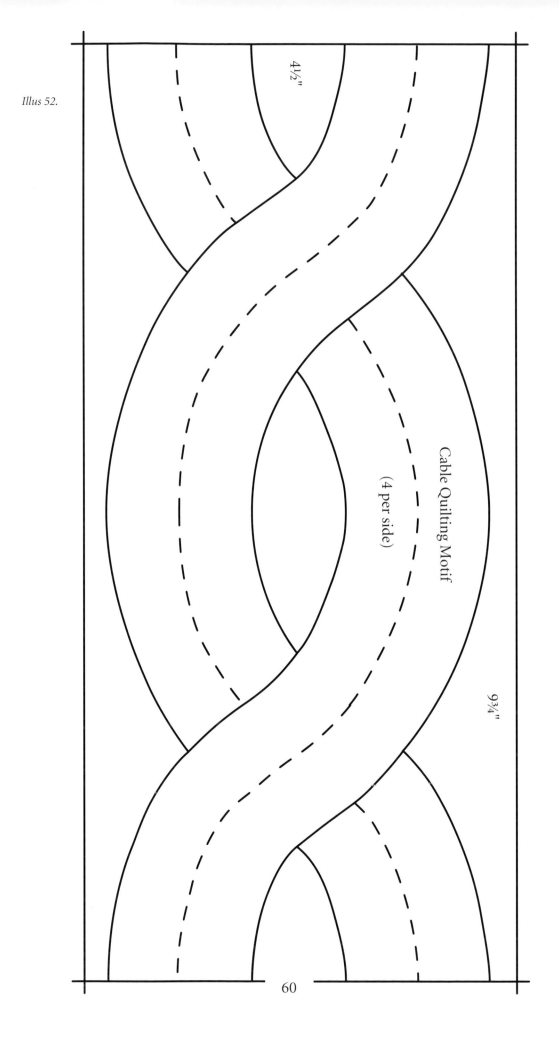

Illus 52.

4½"

Cable Quilting Motif

(4 per side)

9¾"

Canadian Geese in Straw Wreath

42" square

This quilt has won two major awards in international competition and has been published in national magazines. It is especially popular with men.

MATERIALS

- ½ yd green print
- 1¼ yd green solid
- ¾ yd straw calico
- ⅜ yd sky blue
- ¼ yd gray
- ⅛ yd gray print
- ⅞ yd black print
- ¼ yd black & white stripe
- Scraps of yellow
- 1 black embroidery floss
- Water-soluble marker
- Fabric marking pencils
- ¼ yd blue print
- 1½ yd white
- ⅞ yd red
- 1¼ yd backing
- 45" sq. batting
- ⅝ yd black

PATTERN TEMPLATES

Make pattern templates for Arrowhead Border, Zigzag Border, and Water Wheel Border. Refer to *Templates* in *Winning Construction Tips*.

ASSEMBLE QUILT

1. With water-soluble marker, draw 16½" square onto white cotton for center square appliqué; do not cut. On light table, center and trace *Canadian Geese* appliqué onto right side of fabric.

2. On light table, trace each pattern piece for appliqué onto right sides of appropriate fabrics. Cut out, adding ⅛"-¼" seam allowances all around "by eye".

3. Appliqué all pieces with blindstitch. Make French Knot eyes. Optional: with embroidery floss, embroider feet and tail feathers, rather than appliqué.

4. Measure center square again, adjust markings, if necessary, and cut out 16½" square.

5. For corn borders, with rotary cutter and black, cut two 2½" strips across crossgrain of yardage. Further cut these strips into four 18½" strips. Trace corn appliqué patterns onto right sides of yellow and green fabrics. Cut out, as in #2.

Divide 18" (finished) black strips into 2" squares (do not include seam allowances), marking with pins or chalk. Center corn appliqués in 1st, 4th, and 7th squares along each strip. On light table, mark remaining squares with corn pattern for outline quilting. Refer to photo for orientation of placement.

Sew black strips around center square with single butting ends. Press.

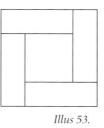

Illus 53.

6. For second border, with rotary cutter, cut two 1" strips across yardage crossgrain of blue print, white, gray print, and straw calico. Sew strips together with ¼" seams, in that order (refer to photo), to create two 2½" wide strips of four fabrics, pressing all seams in one direction. Cut these 4-fabric strips into 4 -2½" squares and 12 -4½" pieces.

With rotary cutter and white, cut 1 -2½" strip across crossgrain. Further cut this stip into 16 -2½" squares. Onto each square trace sheaf of wheat quilting motif, centering design.

Refer to photo to assemble this border. Begin each with a white square (all sheaf of wheat feet will face outward). Press seams. All borders in this quilt face outward, all the way around. Join this border to corn border with single butting ends, as before. Press toward white squares, trimming seam allowances to avoid shadows from behind white.

7. For apple border, with rotary cutter and black print, cut 4 -2½" strips across crossgrain. Further cut these strips into 4 -26½" pieces. Divide each into 12 -2⅟₁₆" long blocks, marking with pins or chalk (do not include seam allowances). Trace apple and leaf motifs onto each 2⅟₁₆" x 2½" block, centering design.

Trace sixteen apple and leaf patterns onto right sides of red and green fabrics. Cut out, as in #2 above. Appliqué apples and leaves onto 1st, 4th, 7th, and 10th blocks on each strip. Join apple border to second border, butting corners as before. Press.

8. For green zigzag border, mark and cut 60C on green print and 120D on white. Piece four equal borders, referring to zigzag pattern block diagram. Press seams toward green. Join these borders to apple border, beginning with a southwest pointing piece C flush with upper right corner of apple border, referring to the photo and the illustration, and butting corners as before. Press.

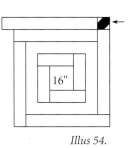

Illus 54.

9. For arrowhead border, mark and cut 68A from blue print, 68B and 68B-reverse from red. Piece four equal borders, pressing seams away from red B toward blue print and away from blue print toward red B-reverse for a sharper blue print point.

Join arrowhead borders to zigzag border, as before. Refer to photo for direction of points. Press.

10. For last border, rotary cut 4 -1" x 37½" strips and 8 -1" x 42½" strips from green.

Mark and cut 144E on straw calico, 144E on white, 72F on white, 144F on green, and 72F on straw calico. Piece four equal borders, referring to *Water Wheel* pattern blocks and pressing seams in alternate directions to reduce bulk and enhance seam matching. Watch placement of F pieces, especially at corners of quilt (see photo). *WATER WHEEL BLOCKS ARE NOT 2" FINISHED.*

Join shorter green strips to arrowhead border, mitering corners. These miters are part of the pieced pattern. Press.

Sew Water Wheel borders to shorter green border, butting corners, refer to photo on page 40. Press.

Join longer green strips to Water Wheel border, mitering corners. Press.

QUILT AND FINISH

1. Baste together the quilt top, batting, and backing. Refer to *Quilting* in *Winning Construction Tips.*

2. Quilt in-the-ditch and along lines drawn already. The quilting would be more balanced with quilted cloud lines behind the geese in the center block.

3. Trim batting and backing edges even with quilt top raw edges.

4. Right sides together, sew remaining four longer green strips to quilt top, mitering corners as fold to the back along seam. Turn under ¼" seam allowances, and blindstitch into place.

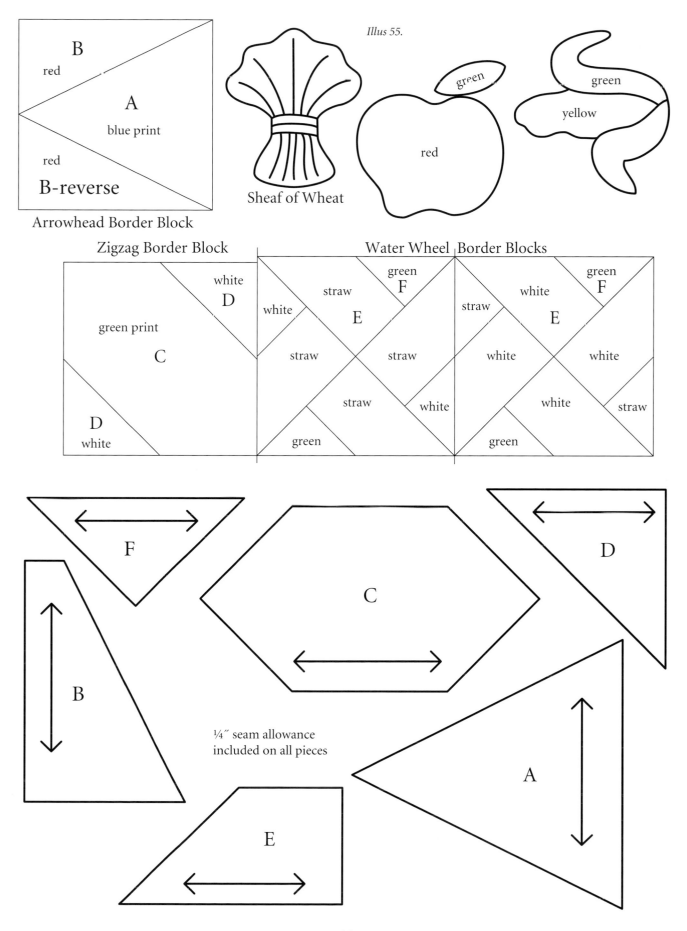

B

red

A

blue print

red

B-reverse

Arrowhead Border Block

Illus 55.

Sheaf of Wheat

green

red

green

yellow

Zigzag Border Block

Water Wheel Border Blocks

white
D

green print

C

D

white

straw

white

green
F

E

straw

straw

straw

green

white

straw

white

green
F

E

straw

white

white

white

green

straw

F

B

C

D

¼″ seam allowance
included on all pieces

E

A

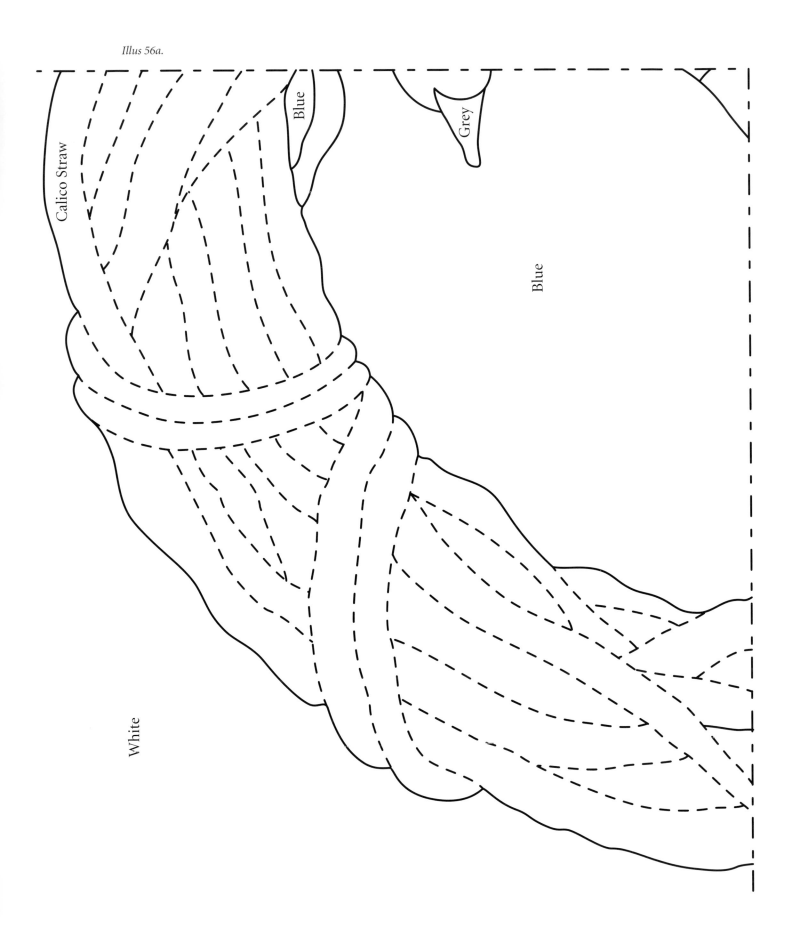

Calico Straw

Blue

Grey

Blue

White

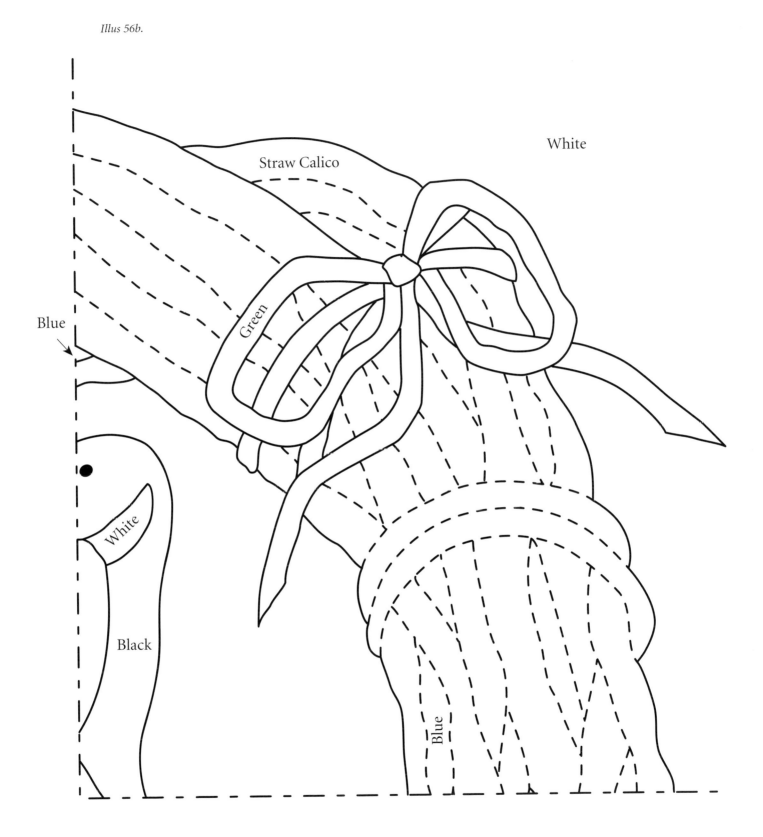

Illus 56b.

White

Straw Calico

Green

Blue

White

Black

Blue

August Pecan and Redbud

40" x 52"

MATERIALS

1" SPEED GRIDS®, optional

3 yd sky blue   • 2 yd tree bark brown

3" x 5" scraps of 41 brown prints for pecan leaves

⅛ yd each of 6 green prints for redbud leaves

1½ yd green print for grass & binding

70" x 80" pin-up sheet

1⅝ yd backing fabric

80-20 batting

Water-soluble marker

PREPARE LEAVES AND TREE TRUNK

1. With 1" SPEED GRIDS®, piece four triangle-blocks from each of 41 brown prints with sky blue, and piece seven triangle-blocks from each of six green prints with sky blue. May use template Z1, if you prefer to mark and cut each fabric in the triangle-blocks. Press seams away from sky blue.

2. This quilt may be either pieced exclusively in 1" horizontal rows (failure-proof, but requiring more time cutting and sewing) or in easy-to-manage horizontal chunks, as I did. This quilt has been left unquilted in the photo in order to illustrate the manner in which I pieced it. After quilting gusts of wind all over the quilt surface, the seam lines will become obliterated.

3. Unless piecing entirely in 1" rows, draw 1" grid onto 40" x 52" vellum. Transfer trunk and tree limb lines onto the grid for appliqué patterns. See *Templates* in *Winning Construction Tips*.

4. To piece entirely in 1" rows, enlarge the entire quilt diagram onto 1" vellum grid, 40" x 52". See *Templates* in *Winning Construction Tips*. This technique would require solid tree trunk fabric.

ASSEMBLE QUILT TOP

1. Hang pin-up sheet from wall or from pole. Find middle of pin-up sheet and middle of quilt diagram. Pin middle triangle-block in place on sheet. Begin pinning triangle-blocks from center moving outward, distributing the prints in a balanced manner over the surface of the quilt top, referring to the quilt diagram for placement. If you do not trust yourself, draw a 1½" grid with a water-soluble marker over the pin-up sheet.

2. With rotary cutter and sky blue, cut strips or rectangles as illustrated on the quilt diagram, adding ¼" seam allowances all around to dimensions before cutting. Make a copy of the quilt diagram on a copy machine in order to outline chunks with a red marker before actual cutting. Outline areas containing many triangle-blocks, then outline unpieced chunks to join those chunks of triangle-blocks. Add these sky blue chunks to the pin-up sheet.

To keep everything manageable, I divided the quilt into about eight unequal horizontal sections. As with all machine piecing, try to routinely sew straight lines from raw edge to raw edge and alternate direction of seam allowances from one row to the next (see *Machine Piecing* in *Winning Construction Tips*). I pieced the entire background ignoring the tree trunk and limb lines since I appliquéd them onto the pieced background. I also ignored the thirty-two pecan leaves and 5½ redbud leaves in front of the tree trunk and limbs to appliqué last.

68

Each redbud leaf consists of two matching triangles and one square. As these triangle-blocks are pinned into position, they will dictate the particular green prints from which to cut 1½" squares (Template S1) to complete leaves. In some cases, part of a leaf is pieced, while part of it is appliquéd. Simply follow the quilt diagram.

3. In addition to the triangle-blocks including sky blue, you will need one brown print and grass green print, three brown print and tree trunk brown,and three green print and tree trunk brown (wait until you know which redbud green prints will be needed). Depending upon the particular arrangement of your leaves, you may or may not need to piece additional triangle-blocks for color balance.

4. When entire background has been pinned to the sheet, sew together into horizontal sections, pressing after joining each row.

5. Trace tree trunk and limbs on light table and appliqué into place. See *Templates* in *Winning Construction Tips*.

6. Distribute 32 pecan leaf triangles and 5½ redbud leaves and leaf parts on top of the tree trunk, limbs, and base, and appliqué into place.

QUILT AND FINISH

1. Baste quilt sandwich, referring to *Quilting* in *Winning Construction Tips*

2. Quilt gusts of wind over entire surface.

3. With rotary cutter and grass green print, cut 2" wide strips on straight of grain to measure 194" when joined by 45° diagonal seams.

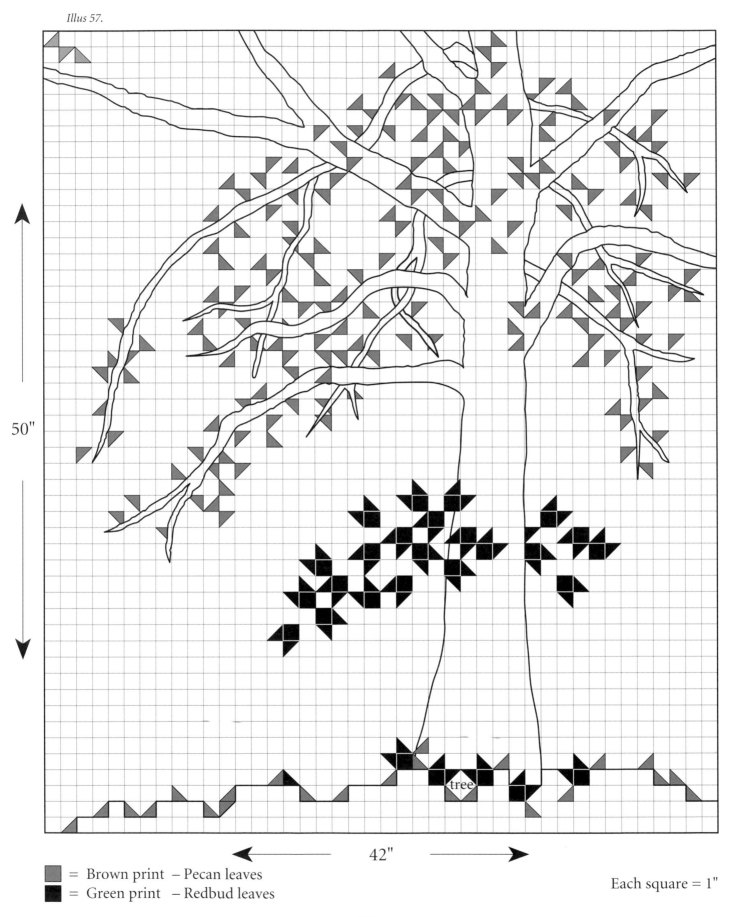

50"

42"

tree

= Brown print – Pecan leaves

= Green print – Redbud leaves

Each square = 1"

Crazy Vest

Sizes 8-10-12-14 16

MATERIALS

1" SPEED GRIDS®, optional

1⅜ yd lightweight fabric for backing

¾ yd polyester lining

Pale pastel scraps of satins and crepe satins

Embroidered cut-outs, Lace cut-outs, Pearl beads

5 Satin-covered ½" bridal buttons

Strip of 5 bridal button loops

3¼ yd ⅛" white satin piping

1¾ yd ¼" pastel satin piping with ⅜" seam allowance

¾ yd flat lace trim for neckline

Assorted decorative buttons, optional

Assorted pastel threads for appliqué and embroidery

Large sheet vellum, tissue, or newsprint

MAKE OWN PIPING

⅛" satin piping is available in fabric stores. For ¼" piping with ⅜" seam allowance, cut bias strips 1½" wide. Sew ends of strips together with 45° diagonal seams into total length of 63". Press seams open. Fold strip in half, wrong sides together, with ⁵⁄₃₂" piping cord along inside fold. With piping foot or zipper foot, stitch close to cord.

PATTERN PIECES

Carefully remove FRONT and BACK VEST pattern pages from back, tracing one side of each page onto vellum. Trace appropriate size of each piece onto vellum and cut out.

MAKE CRAZY-PATCHED FABRIC

1. In order to prevent reducing the finished vest size from possible take-up when patches are sewn onto vest backing, cut backing fabric in half along crosswise fold parallel to raw edges. Draw outlines of one VEST FRONT and one VEST BACK onto these two rectangles (for guidelines in placement of patchwork and other special adornments). Mark shoulder line on back button extension.

2. Piece patchwork pattern blocks using satins and crepe satins of your choice. Drawings of some possibilities are included below. Patterns for the *Pine Tree* block and the *Grape Basket* block may be found with *Plaid Love-Apple Tree* and *MiniatureGrape Basket*. Piecing is much easier and much faster using the 1" SPEED GRIDS® since they totally stabilize these slippery fabrics and eliminate dealing with ravelling satin edges, distortions, and tiny triangles. I have even used them with knit suedecloth on a pieced vest. Denim is a good choice, too (*see Machine Piecing* in *Winning Construction Tips*).

Rotary cut the squares and rectangles, adding seam allowances before cutting, to complete the pattern blocks. *(See Machine Piecing* in *Winning Construction Tips.)*

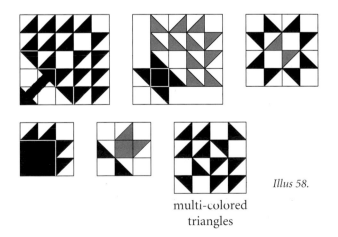

Illus 58.

multi-colored
triangles

3. Place pieced blocks in pleasing, balanced arrangement over the drawn outlines of VEST FRONT and VEST BACK on backing fabric, right sides up.

4. Add irregular scraps of satin and crepe satin to fill in the remaining empty areas on the backing fabric, making sure to include ¼" seam allowances all around. Overlap drawn outlines of VEST FRONT and BACK with the patches. It may be helpful to sew two to four scraps together with ¼" seams before sewing them onto the backing fabric.

Another way to add scraps is to begin with a pattern block or scrap pinned into place, right side up, on the backing fabric. Place another scrap on top of the first, right sides together, raw edges even. Sew ¼" seam through all layers. Finger press newly added scrap into place. Add next scrap in same manner.

Illus 59a.

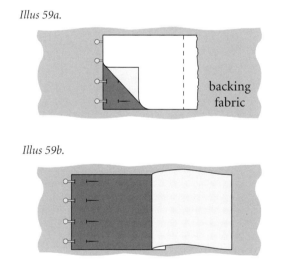

backing fabric

Illus 59b.

Many edges may need to be turned under and blindstitched into place, as in appliqué. Be sure to stop stitching ¼" from folded edge (½" from raw edge) for room to turn under seam allowance.

5. When VEST FRONT and VEST BACK surfaces have been covered with crazy patches, redraw vest outlines over the crazy patch. This will provide a guide within which to embroider along the seamlines. Do not forget

to mark the shoulder line on the back button extension again. (The embroidery could produce some take-up in the fabric, so the vest pieces should not be cut out at this time.)

6. Apply novelty trims, buttons, and/or beads.

7. To embroider the decorative stitches over the seamlines, I used decorative stitches on my sewing machine. They look hand-done but were completed in a fraction of the time.

An alternative to machine embroidery is hand embroidery using two stands of embroidery floss. Below is a small sample of possible stitches to use.

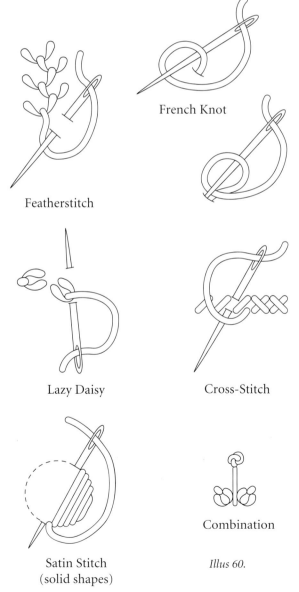

French Knot

Featherstitch

Lazy Daisy

Cross-Stitch

Satin Stitch (solid shapes)

Combination

Illus 60.

72

8. When all adornments have been added to the vest surfaces, make sure the VEST FRONT and BACK are still true to size, and cut out.

ASSEMBLE VEST

Note seam allowances: side and shoulder seams are ⅝". Armhole and neck edges are ¼". Outside edge is ⅜".

1. With right sides together and raw edges even, sew ⅝" non-button shoulder seam. Trim seam to ¼". Finger press seam open. Embroider over seams, catching seam allowances on either side of seamline with embroidery stitches.

2. Baste flat lace trim to vest neck edge along ¼" seamline.

3. With zipper foot, baste ⅛" white satin piping to neckline's ¼" seamline (raw edges even).

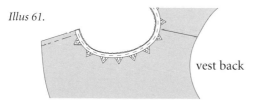

Illus 61.

vest back

4. With right sides together and raw edges even, sew ⅝" underarm seam. Trim seam to ¼". Finger press seam open. Embroider over seam, catching seam allowances on either side of seamline with embroidery stitches.

5. With zipper foot, baste ⅛" white satin piping to armhole edge on ¼" seamline (raw edges even). Begin with piping end extended into seam allowance at underarm seam. Finish in the same manner. Trim piping ends flush with raw edge.

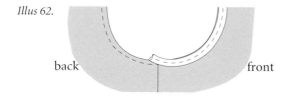

Illus 62.

back   front

6. With zipper foot, baste ⅛" white satin piping onto top of ¼" pastel satin piping with white covered cording resting against pastel covered cording. Stitch over previously stitched line on white piping.

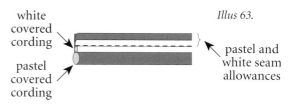

white covered cording

pastel covered cording

Illus 63.

pastel and white seam allowances

7. With zipper foot, baste double piping along outside edge of vest, right sides together, from one open shoulder edge to the other, raw edges even, stitching over seamline closest to raw edges.

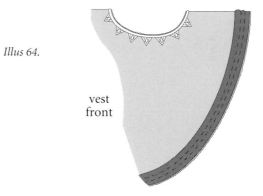

Illus 64.

vest front

8. Center bridal button loops chain over ⅝" seamline on open-shoulder front edge. Stitch into place. (Pipings should face outward.)

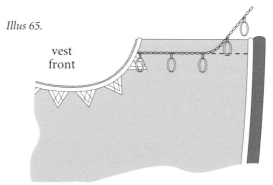

Illus 65.

vest front

9. Using wrong sides of VEST FRONT and VEST BACK pattern pieces, cut out lining.

10. With lining pieces right sides together and raw edges even, sew ⅝" non-button shoulder and side seams. Trim seams to ¼". Press open.

11. With right sides together and raw edges even, sew lining to vest along basting lines on vest from front open-shoulder edge along ¼" neckline seamline, 2" from raw shoulder edge, to within 2" of back open-shoulder raw edge at neckline. (This prevents sewing pipings down in wrong position.) Sew ⅝" seam across back open-shoulder edge between ¼" neckline seamline and ⅜" vest outside edge seamline, making sure not to catch pipings in seam.

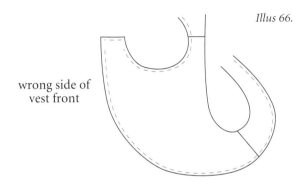

Illus 66.

wrong side of vest front

Begin sewing again 2" from open-shoulder button-extension raw edge with ⅜" seam (along basted line closest to raw edge) around entire outside edge of vest to within 2" of front open-shoulder raw edge. Sew ⅝" seam across front open-shoulder edge between ¼" neckline seamline and ⅜" vest outside edge seamline, making sure not to catch pipings in seam. Clip curves at neckline and armhole.

12. Turn vest right side out through armhole opening.

13. Turn under lining seam allowance around armhole and at open-shoulder corners, and blindstitch into place.

14. By hand, tack lining to crazy-patch backing fabric ¼" from all outside edges to prevent its rolling out.

15. Line up front open-shoulder edge along marked shoulder line on back button-extension. Mark button placement. Sew on buttons.

Black Magnolia

84" square

This quilt has won a major award in international competition, been juried and invited into various international exhibits, and been featured in national magazines. In spite of its 1217 pieces, it took only 80 hours to piece with 3" SPEED GRIDS®! Complete patterns and instructions are included here, as well as patterns for the **4"** miniature pieced block made from scraps and incorporated into a handbag, as seen in Photo # 13.

MATERIALS

3" SPEED GRIDS®, optional

1¼ yd each of 6 neutral background solids

⅜ yd white for stars and 8 border triangles

¾ yd black for border triangles

½ yd for set of four arrowheads in *each* pattern block

⅛ yd for set of 8 triangles around the center square in *each* pattern block

⅛ yd for set of four small squares in *each* pattern block

7" square for center square in *each* pattern block

2¾ yd 90" bleached muslin for four squares in center of four white stars and for 90" square backing

90" square 80/20 batting

¼" drafting tape

Light gray and Ecru quilting threads

84" Square   Each square = 3"   Plain squares in backround and borders = triangle-blocks

Illus 68.

Quilting Diagram

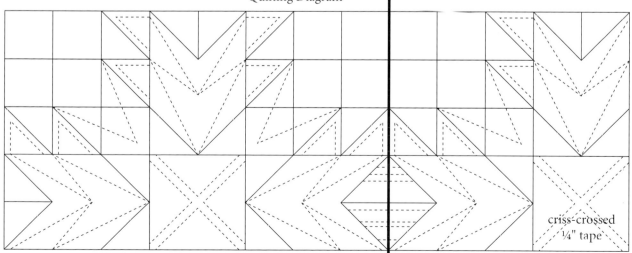

criss-crossed
¼" tape

PATTERN TEMPLATES

3" SPEED GRIDS®, Z3, S3, S5, S6, and Arrowhead. Refer to *Templates* in *Winning Constructions Tips.*

MARK FABRICS

Using 3" SPEED GRIDS® or template Z3:

346 triangle-blocks in random combinations, neutral solids

87 triangle-blocks in random neutral solids and black

37 triangle-blocks in random neutral solids and white

3 triangle-blocks black and white

88 triangles random neutral solids

4 squares Template S5 from bleached muslin

ASSEMBLE PATTERN BLOCK

1. Refer to *General Pattern Block Piecing Diagram* and the whole quilt diagram as lay out pieces for each pattern block: four Arrowheads, four squares S3, one square S6, eight triangles Z3, eight triangles Z3 random neutrals, thirty-two triangle-blocks in random neutral combinations.

Be aware of the pattern blocks which have the inclusion of triangle-blocks with black and for white star pieces, marked with a dot (•). Check for random distribution of background neutrals and directions of diagonal seamlines.

2. Helpful Hints: a) Mark seam allowances at points marked in illustration on wrong side of fabric. b) Snip to within one thread of seam allowance at point marked with arrow, and sew by hand 1" to either side of that point; then continue machine-piecing. c) A sharper point at the tip of the arrowhead will be

achieved if one Triangle Z3 seam allowance is pressed toward the arrowhead and one Triangle Z3 seam allowance is pressed toward Triangle Z3. d) Press seams of background triangle-block rows in alternating directions (see *Machine Piecing* in *Winning Construction Tips*).

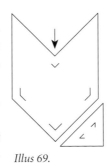

Illus 69.

Illus 70.

Gereral Pattern Block Piecing Diagram

3. The muslin square in the middle of each white star, plus the random neutral triangles Z3 on each side of the muslin square, should be set aside and set-in as the nine pattern blocks are joined later. Leave ¼" free in seams where the square will be added.

4. Join pieces into rows. Join rows into squares. Press seams in top and bottom thirds of pattern block away from arrowhead piece. Press seams in middle third toward center square.

ASSEMBLE QUILT

1. Refer to whole quilt diagram, and lay out all nine pattern blocks. Check to be sure four complete white stars are in their proper places.

2. Sew three rows of pattern blocks, then sew these rows into a 72" (finished) square.

3. Refer to whole quilt diagram again, and lay out double triangle-block rows for borders. Check again for random distribution of neutrals. Border blocks with a white triangle are marked with a dot.

4. Sew two short borders to opposite sides of quilt top. Sew two long borders to top and bottom of quilt top.

QUILT AND FINISH

1. Mark magnolia bud quilting motif in center square of four white stars with tops of buds radiating from center of quilt.

2. Trim away any black seam raw edges that extend beyond pale seam raw edges to avoid shadows behind pale pieces. Trim any dark threads for the same reason.

3. Baste quilt top, batting, and backing with batting and backing extending an equal distance beyond all sides. See *Quilting* in *Winning Construction Tips.*

4. All Triangles and pattern block pieces are outline quilted in-the-ditch. I used ecru quilting thread in the background areas and light gray around the 9 pattern blocks' pattern. I also used light gray around the black triangles in the borders.

5. Use ¼" drafting tape to mark quilting lines to enhance a star-like appearance in the 9 pattern blocks (see *Quilting Diagram*). Randomly-spaced straight lines appear between arrowheads, where the pattern blocks come together ONLY.

6. When finish quilting, trim batting even with quilt top. Trim backing ¾" beyond quilt top. Turn backing to the inside ¼", then fold toward front of quilt, blind-stitching along imaginary ¼" seam and mitering corners.

4" PATTERN BLOCK

Refer to *General Pattern Block Piecing Diagram* and use ½" SPEED GRIDS® with templates Z, S, S1, and Arrowhead template, below. Scraps of fabric are enough for each block.

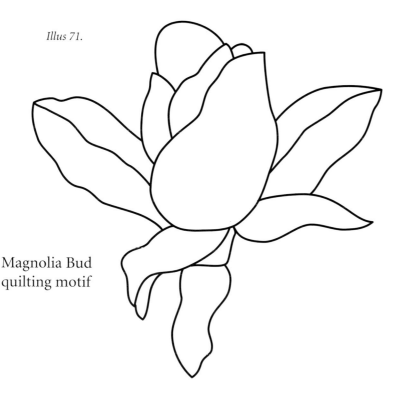

Illus 71.

Magnolia Bud quilting motif

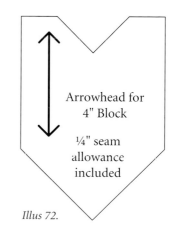

Arrowhead for 4" Block

¼" seam allowance included

Illus 72.

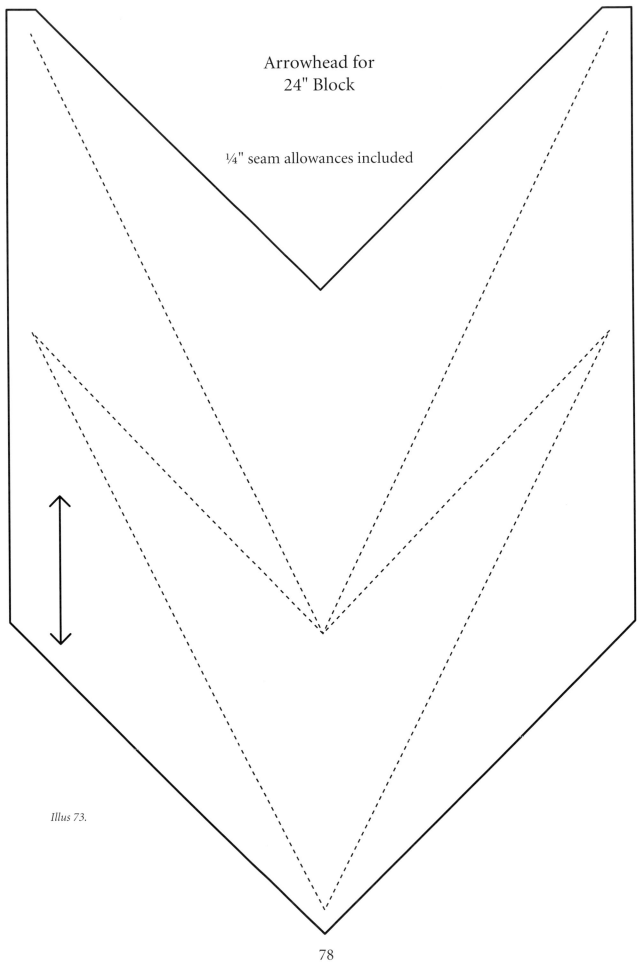

Arrowhead for
24" Block

¼" seam allowances included

Illus 73.

Amish English Ivy

84" square

This pattern is an excellent manner of joining imperfect pattern blocks, such as those won at a quilt event or bought at a flea market. Following complete instructions and patterns for the 84" quilt with **12"** pattern blocks are patterns for the 3" and 6" pattern blocks. While the **3"** block is perfect for miniatures and clothing, the **6"** block would be great in clothing, crib quilts, borders, and wall-hangings, besides being quite stunning in a full size quilt.

Variation: 16 pattern blocks, all set "on point", substituting plain blocks in rows with three pattern blocks (see *Quilt Diagram*) and eliminating sashing strips.

MATERIALS

2" SPEED GRIDS®, optional

¼ yd scraps for *each* of the 25 pattern blocks – all solids, no white, no muslin, with three to nine colors per pattern block

2 yd peach

3¼ yd turquoise

2¾ yd 90" backing

90" square 80/20 batting

⅝ yd turquoise binding

Freezer paper or contact paper

PATTERN TEMPLATES

See *Templates* in *Winning Construction Tips* and prepare templates Z2 (unless using 2" SPEED GRIDS®), Z4, R10, S4, and S6.

For peach border templates: Draw right triangle with 10.6" sides (see drafting ruler in *Pattern Templates* section) and 15" diagonal. Add ¼" seam allowances all around.

Draw 15" right triangle. Add ¼" seam allowances. Grainline should be on the diagonal.

ASSEMBLE PATTERN BLOCK

1. With 2" SPEED GRIDS® or template Z2, piece nine triangle-blocks with colors of your choice (refer to *Basic Piecing Diagram*).

2. Join quarters of the pattern block into 6" (finished) squares (refer to *Machine-Piecing* in *Winning Construction Tips*). Press seams in each "row" in alternating directions.

3. For stem in square S6, cut 1" x 9" bias strip. Fold in half, wrong sides together; sew ¼" seam; trim close to stitching. Center seam under this ¼" tube, and appliqué into place.

Next, sew one triangle Z2 to bottom corner of this 6½" square. Line up raw bias edge, right sides together, with "raw edge" line marked on pattern piece S6. Sew ¼" seam (sewing over raw edge of appliquéd stem). Trim away background corner.

4. Join the four 6½" squares into pairs, then into one 12" (finished) square.

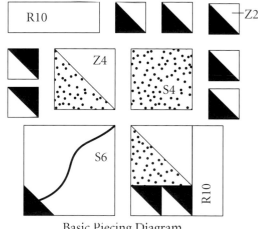

Basic Piecing Diagram

Illus 74.

Frame Pattern Blocks

1. With rotary cutter and turquoise, cut four 14" wide (14½", if working with imperfect blocks) strips across crosswise grain of yardage. Reserve remaining, in case you need to cut another, depending on actual workable width of the fabric.

2. Cut these strips further into 100 -2" x 14" (2½" x 14½", if imperfect blocks) pieces.

3. Refer to *Block Framing Diagram* and join turquoise strips to pattern blocks. Framing the blocks in this man-ner, rather than with two short and two long strips, avoids unmatched seams when joining the framed blocks into the quilt top, par-ticularly when using imperfect blocks. Press.

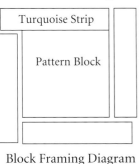

Turquoise Strip

Pattern Block

Block Framing Diagram
Illus 75.

4. Trim framed pattern blocks with 15½" square (15" finished) template, if using imperfect blocks only.

Assemble Quilt Top

1. Refer to *Peach Layout Diagram*, and mark and cut twelve 15" (finished) triangles and four 10.6" (finished) triangles.

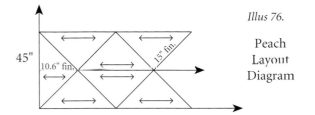

Illus 76.

45"

10.6" fin.

15" fin.

Peach Layout Diagram

2. Refer to whole quilt diagram and join framed pattern blocks and peach triangles into diagonal rows. Press seams in alternating rows in opposite directions.

3. Join diagonal rows. Press.

Quilt and Finish

1. Baste and quilt sandwich following directions in *Quilting* in *Winning Construction Tips*.

2. Outline each piece of the ivy in the pattern block by quilting in-the-ditch.

3. Trace each *English Ivy* quilting motif onto freezer paper or contact paper twenty-five to fifty times (enough for $\frac{1}{16}$-$\frac{1}{8}$ portion of the quilt at a time).

4. Distribute motifs in turquoise areas to either side of an as yet imaginary ¼" vining stem. Also place motifs in open areas in pattern blocks, especially in square S6. Be sure to place a motif at each intersection of the turquoise "frames".

5. In peach areas, arrange *English Ivy* motifs to cover in the same density as the rest of the quilt top.

6. Quilt around the *English Ivy* motifs. By eye, connect leaves with ¼" wide vining stems. Add a squiggle for tendrils wherever a little too much space remains unquilted.

7. For binding, with rotary cutter and turquoise, cut nine 2" wide strips across crossgrain of yardage. Join strips with 45° diagonal seams. See *Finishing* in *Winning Construction Tips*.

3" Pattern Block

Refer to *Basic Piecing Diagram* and use ½" SPEED GRIDS® with templates Z, Z1, S1 S1.5, and R1.

6" Pattern Block

Refer to *Basic Piecing Diagram* and use 1" SPEED GRIDS® with templates Z1, Z2, S2, S3, and R4. ⅛ yard scraps will be enough for each of the pattern blocks.

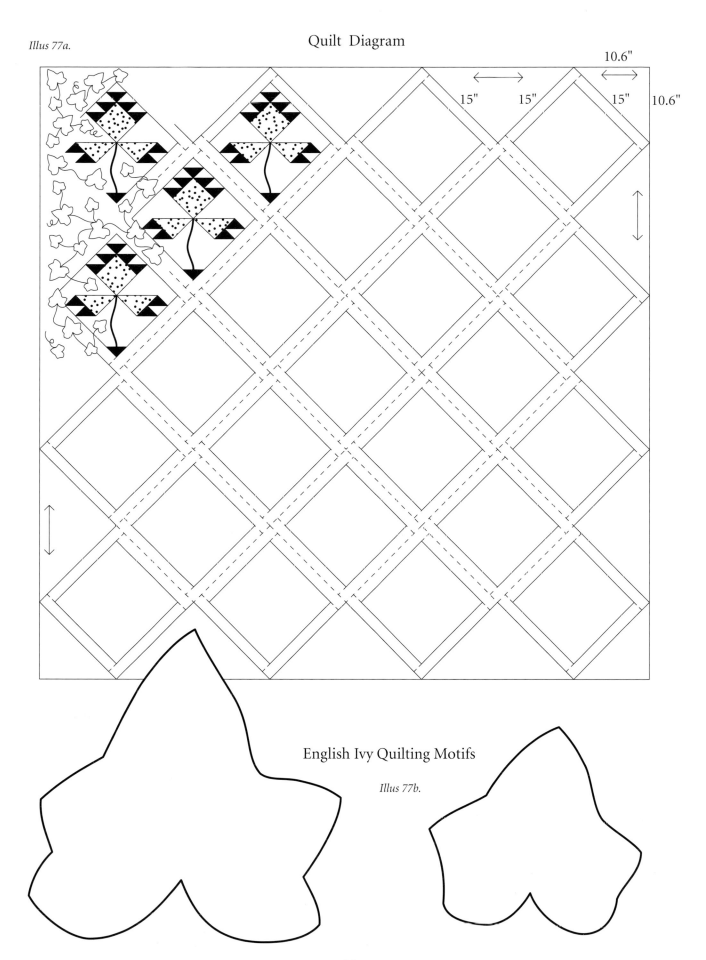

Illus 77a.

10.6"

15" 15" 15" 10.6"

English Ivy Quilting Motifs

Illus 77b.

Miniature Grape Basket

17½" square

The *Grape Basket* pattern block remains one of my favorites because it has enough triangles to treat the block with a variety of appearances based upon color alone. Below are complete instructions and patterns for the 17½" miniature quilt using **2½"** pattern blocks. Following, find patterns for the **5"** (see Photo #6 and Photo #10) and **10"** pattern blocks. Although the **5"** block is perfect for clothing, it is also a great choice for a crib quilt, wallhanging, or border. The **10"** block is a good size to use in a bed quilt.

MATERIALS

½" SPEED GRIDS®, optional

1" SPEED GRIDS®, optional

¹⁄₁₆-⅛ yd (scraps) of eleven fabrics (from which one to three should be contrasting; I chose red, white, and black)

1 yd background fabric (turquoise)

¼ yd binding fabric (red)

21" square 80/20 batting

⅝ yd backing fabric

PIECE 2½" PATTERN BLOCK

For random scrappy appearance in the 16 pattern blocks, with ½" SPEED GRIDS® or Template Z, piece 16-24 triangle-blocks each from eleven fabrics and background fabric (16 each of contrast colors; 24 of most colors; will need a total of 208 triangle-blocks for the pattern blocks). With 1" SPEED GRIDS® or Template Z1, piece 2 triangle-blocks each from eleven fabrics with background color for basket bases.

With rotary cutter and single layer background color, cut 32 -1" squares (½" fin.) and 32 -1" x 2" rectangles, or use Templates Z and R1, if you prefer.

Refer to *Pattern Block Piecing Diagram* to first join pieces into rows for a 2" square; join the rows, then piece the strips which join to the 2" square to form a 2½" square. It is very important to alternate seam allowances from one row to the next when working on such a small scale (see *Machine Piecing* in *Winning Construction Tips*).

Piece 12 blocks with any color combinations you prefer. Pin up on a wall and arrange as you go. For last 4 blocks, choose color combinations which balance the rest.

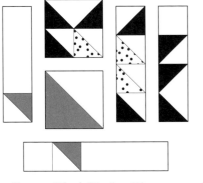

Pattern Block Piecing Diagram   *Illus 78.*

ASSEMBLE QUILT

1. With rotary cutter and background fabric, cut 1 -11" square. Cut 8 -2.64" squares (see drafting ruler on page 95), then cut each on the diagonal to create 16 -1.77" (finished) right triangles with 2½" (finished) diagonal for Piece A.

Cut twelve 3⅜" squares, then cut each on the diagonal to create 24 -2½" (finished) right triangles for Piece B.

2. Refer to *Quilting Diagram* and join pieces A and B to the pattern blocks to be in the 2 short borders. Join these 2 borders to opposite sides of the center square. Press.

3. Join pieces A and B to the pattern blocks that will be in the two longer borders. Join these two borders to the top and bottom of the quilt top. Press.

QUILT AND FINISH

1. Fold quilt top in half both horizontally and vertically to crease guide lines for the quilting motif in the center of the quilt. On a light table, with a water-soluble marker, trace the central motif, one quarter at a time.

2. Working on such a small scale , I lost a lot of details behind seam allowances in the corners of the quilting design of the remaining central areas over the light table. To solve this problem, I traced the larger quilting motif onto clear template material and cut it out. Then I was able to easily mark around it with a water-soluble marker, one quarter of the remaining area at a time.

3. In the 2½" triangles along the outside edge of the quilt, I marked around the tip of the quilting stencil I made, as illustrated in one of the triangles in the *Quilting Diagram*. In the four outside corners of the quilt, I marked the tiny portion of the tip of the quilting stencil, as indicated with a dotted line on that design.

4. Baste the three layers of the quilt together. See *Quilting* in *Winning Construction Tips*.

5. Quilt along marked lines by hand or with free-motion machine quilting (refer to *Machine Quilting* in *Winning Construction Tips*). In each pattern block, quilt in-the-ditch outlining each colored pattern piece.

6. With rotary cutter and red, cut 2" wide strips across the width of the yardage to produce a length of 80" when joined with 45° diagonal seams. See *Finishing* in *Winning Construction Tips*.

Quilt Diagram

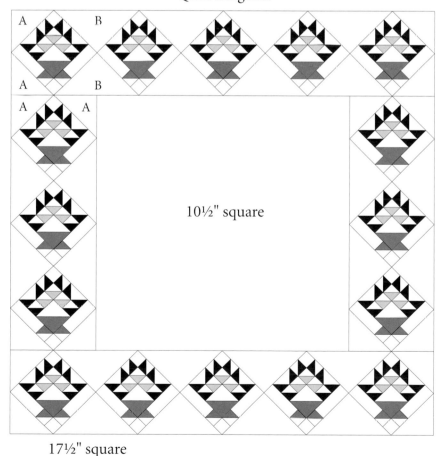

A B

A B

A A

10½" square

Illus 79.

17½" square

83

Pattern
Block

Pattern
Block

Pattern
Block

Pattern
Block

Pattern
Block

FOLD

FOLD

Illus 80.

5" PATTERN BLOCK

1. For each block, with 1" SPEED GRIDS® or template Z1, piece eleven triangle-blocks to be placed above basket base and two triangle-blocks to be part of the basket base in color combinations of your choice with the background color. With 2" SPEED GRIDS® or template Z2, piece one triangle-block for the basket base with the background color (refer to Photos 6, 10, 13).

2. With rotary cutter and background color, cut two 1½" squares (1" finished) and two 1½" x 3½" rectangles, or use templates S1 and R4, if you prefer.

3. Refer to *Pattern Block Piecing Diagram* to join pieces into pattern block.

4. For 35⅓" crib quilt, refer to ASSEMBLE QUILT above. Use template Z3.5 for piece A, template Z5 for piece B, and cut 21¾" center square (21¼" finished). Although not important in the 17½" quilt, be sure to place the diagonal of template Z5 on the straight of the grain of the fabric.

5. To sew this block in denim, as in Photo #6, refer to *Machine Piecing* in *Winning Construction Tips*.

10" PATTERN BLOCK

1. For each block, with 2" SPEED GRIDS® or templates Z2 and Z4, piece triangle-blocks as for 5" pattern block above.

2. With rotary cutter and background color, cut two 2½" squares (2" finished) and two 2½" x 6½" rectangles, or use templates S2 and R10.

3. Refer to *Pattern Block Piecing Diagram* to join pieces into pattern block.

4. For 70.70" quilt, refer to ASSEMBLE QUILT above. Cut 43" center square (42½" finished). For template A, draw 7.07" right triangle (see drafting ruler in *Pattern Templates* section) with 10" diagonal; add ¼" seam allowances all around. For template B, draw 10" right triangle with 14.14" diagonal; add ¼" seam allowances all around. Grainline should be on the diagonal on template B.

5. Heavily quilted grape vines with hanging clusters of grapes, perhaps stuffed, and closely quilted lattice strips would be excellent choices for the quilting in the central unpieced areas.

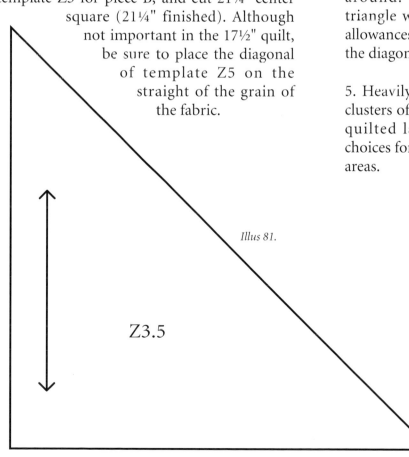

Illus 81.

Z3.5

Christmas Ribbons

47¾" square

This pieced ribbon setting lends itself to framing anything of special interest to the quilter. I chose to appliqué a drawing of Santa by my then four-year-old daughter. A pattern for the appliqué was easily made by enlarging the drawing to 14" on a copy machine.

A flowery appliqué block would be beautiful, as would a heavily quilted special design. Requirements for 3½" and 7" blocks follow instructions for the quilt with the 14" blocks.

The **3½"** blocks would be perfect for a miniature quilt or apparel. The **7"** block would be great as a border.

MATERIALS

2" SPEED GRIDS®, optional

2¼ yd gray

1½ yd dark teal

½ yd red print

For appliqué:

Scraps of pink, turquoise, yellow, royal blue, brown, and red with ⅛ yd of white

52" square 80/20 batting

1½ yd 90" wide backing

PIECE 14" PATTERN BLOCK

1. For each block, with 2" SPEED GRIDS® or template Z2, piece twelve triangle-blocks red print and gray and six triangle-blocks dark teal and gray.

2. For each block: With rotary cutter and gray, cut two 2½" squares, four 2½" x 4½" rectangles, and one 4½" x 10½" rectangle. From dark teal, cut four 2½" squares. From red print, cut seven 2½" squares. Templates S2, R7, and R11 may be used, if preferred.

3. Referring to piecing diagram, sew portions of three horizontal rows of the pattern block. Join portions into three horizontal rows, and sew the 3 horizontal rows into a 14½" square (14" finished). Alternate directions of seam allowances from one row to the next (see *Machine Piecing* in *Winning Construction Tips*).

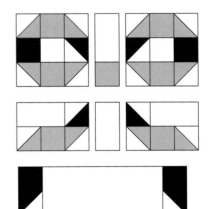

Pattern Block Piecing Diagram   *Illus 82.*

APPLIQUÉ CENTER

If appliquéing a 14" block, do so now. If appliquéing a design which flows beyond the confines of the 14" square, do so after assembling quilt top.

In my appliqué, I embroidered areas which were very small; such as, the reindeer's face and harness, the window pane dividers, the door knob, and Santa's arms, legs, and face.

ASSEMBLE QUILT

1. With rotary cutter and gray, cut five 14½" squares (14" finished) and four borders, 3⅜" x 48¼". Cut the borders on the straight of the

grain to avoid ruffled edges. Make a 14½" square template, if you prefer.

2. Refer to *Quilt Diagram* and join pieced and solid blocks into three horizontal rows; join the three rows into one square.

3. Join gray borders to the 42" (fin.) square, mitering corners (see *Finishing* in *Winning Construction Tips*).

QUILT AND FINISH

1. Baste together the quilt top, batting, and backing. Refer to *Quilting* in *Winning Construction Tips*.

2. I quilted around all the appliqué pieces in the center and outlined my daughter's hand-drawn stars in the background. Since the stars did not stand out as much as I wanted, I painted over them with silver sparkle paint. I also tied French knots of white "snow" in the central area through all layers. Surrounding the appliquéd center, I quilted a diagonal grid over the remaining surface of the quilt, which explains the odd width of the gray border. It would look even better with Christmas wreaths quilted in the plain blocks.

3. With a rotary cutter and dark teal, cut 2" wide strips to produce a length of 200" when joined with 45° diagonal seams. Refer to *Finishing* in *Winning Construction Tips*.

3½" PATTERN BLOCK

1. Each block needs about ⅛ yd each of red, dark teal, and gray.

2. For each block, with ½" SPEED GRIDS® or template Z, piece triangle-blocks as in #1 for 14" blocks.

3. For each block: with rotary cutter and gray, cut two 1" squares, four 1" x 1½" rectangles, and one 1½" x 3" rectangle. From dark teal,

cut four 1" squares. From red print, cut seven 1" squares. May use templates S, R, and R3.

4. Continue from #3 in 14" blocks, above.

7" PATTERN BLOCK

1. Each block needs about ⅛ yd each of red, dark teal, and gray.

2. For each block, with 1" SPEED GRIDS® or template Z1, piece triangle-blocks as in #1 for 14" blocks.

3. For each block: with rotary cutter and gray, cut two 1½" squares, four 1½" x 2½ rectangles, and one 2½" x 5½" rectangle. From dark teal, cut four 1½" squares. From red, cut seven 1½" squares. May use templates S1, R2, and R9.

4. Continue from #3 in 14 " blocks, above.

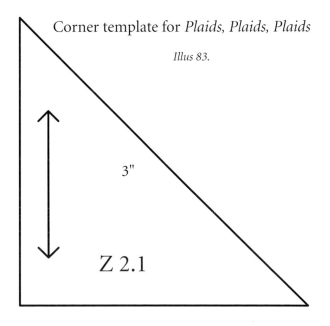

Corner template for *Plaids, Plaids, Plaids*

Illus 83.

3"

Z 2.1

Quilt Diagram

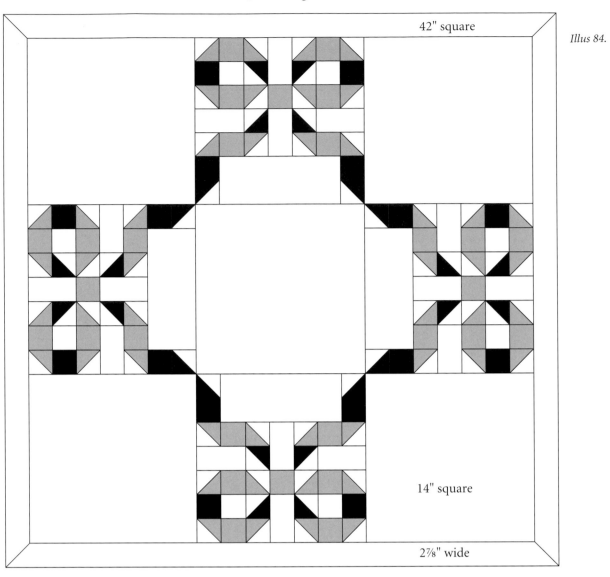

42" square

Illus 84.

14" square

2⅞" wide

47¾"

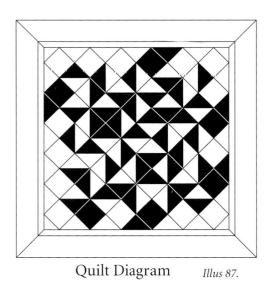

Quilt Diagram   *Illus 87.*

Plaids, Plaids, Plaids

39⅝" square

Piece this project in one day, machine quilt it in one more!

MATERIALS

3" SPEED GRIDS®, optional

Scraps of 13 dark plaids

Scraps of 13 light plaids

1 yd red solid

1½ yd final border (or more, to accommodate specific plaid repeats)

80/20 batting

1½ yd small red and white checked backing

approx. 40" square pin-up sheet

ASSEMBLE QUILT TOP

1. Piece 41 triangle-blocks with dark plaid and light plaid, varying the combinations, with 3" SPEED GRIDS® or with Template Z3. Piece 6 triangle-blocks with two dark plaids and 14 triangle-blocks with two light plaids. With Template Z3, cut five triangles from dark plaid and 15 triangles from light plaid. With Template Z2.1(page 87), cut four light triangles.

2. Refer to *Quilt Diagram* and pin triangle-blocks and triangles to pin-up sheet. Check for balanced distribution of particular darks and lights. (All squares = triangles-blocks.)

3. Sew triangle-blocks and triangles together in diagonal rows, alternating directions of seam allowances from one row to the next (see *Machine Piecing* in *Winning Construction Tips*). Sew diagonal rows into 24⅝" square, finished.

4. Cut four red borders, 2" x 28⅛" (1½" x 27⅝" finished). Sew to plaid square, mitering corners (refer to *Finishing* in *Winning Construction Tips*).

5. The final border is 6" wide (finished) with an additional 1¼" turned to the back side of the quilt. Cut four strips 7½" x 42⅛". Join to red borders, mitering corners. Baste a line 6" from the red border all around.

QUILT AND FINISH

1. For a different twist, I chose to quilt a copy machine enlargement of a photo of my children in the plaid center of this quilt (see *Machine Quilting* in *Winning Construction Tips* for details). I also quilted in-the-ditch around the red border and quilted my children's handprints in the final 6" border. See Illus. 86.

2. After quilting, trim batting and backing to the basted line in final border. Fold 1¼" to back side of quilt, mitering corners; turn under ¼" and blindstitch into place.

3. This would be a fun quilt to tea-dye overall to look like it had been found in the attic! Put a truthful label on the back of it, though, for the benefit of your descendants!

4. This would be a great quilt blown up to 6" triangle-blocks, with each triangle string-pieced or crazy-patched.

Chintz Ruffled Pillow

28" square + ruffles

Two of these pillows provide a perfect headboard on a double or queen-size bed. One looks great in a wicker or an overstuffed chair, or with a collection of pillows.

MATERIALS

2" SPEED GRIDS®, optional

¼ yd yellow solid

¼ yd green solid

¾ yd pink for corded piping

1½ yd chintz

1¼ yd pink and white stripe

7 yd 5" eyelet ruffle

3½ yd ³⁄₁₆" piping cord

Purchased or self-made 28" stuffed pillow form

1 yd muslin backing (or matching chintz)

PIECE 20" PATTERN BLOCK

1. With 2" SPEED GRIDS® or Template Z2, piece: 24 triangle-blocks yellow and chintz; 8 triangle-blocks yellow and green; 8 triangle-blocks green and chintz.

2. With rotary cutter and yellow, cut eight 2½" squares. With chintz, cut twelve 2½" squares, one 4½" square, and four 6½" squares, or may use Templates S2, S4, and S6.

3. Referring to piecing diagram (each square = 2"), piece three rows of three squares or rectangles each, then join the three rows into the 20" finished pattern block. See *Machine Piecing* in *Winning Construction Tips*.

ASSEMBLE PILLOW

1. With rotary cutter and pink solid, cut 1⅞" wide bias strips to total 112" in length when joined by 45° diagonal seams. Press seams open. With piping or cording foot, enclose ³⁄₁₆" piping cord in the bias strip, leaving a ⅝" seam allowance.

2. With rotary cutter and pink and white stripe, cut 6¼" wide strips to total 224" when joined in ¼" seams. Be careful not to interrupt striped pattern with seams. Press seams open. Fold wrong sides together, and line up raw edges with raw edge of eyelet ruffle. Sew gathering seam ⅝" from all three raw edges.

3. With rotary cutter and chintz, cut two pieces 4⅞" x 20½" and two pieces 4⅞" x 29¼". This will allow ⅝" seam allowances around the outside edge of the 28" finished square, in order to make it easier to join piping and ruffles. Sew the two shorter pieces to opposite sides of the 20" (finished) pattern block. Sew the two longer pieces to the top and the bottom of the pattern block.

4. Sew piping to 28" square with ⅝" seams.

5. Gather ruffles along gathering thread and sew right on top of ⅝" piping seam, distributing gathers evenly along each side of pillow square.

6. From muslin, cut one piece 16½" x 29¼". Finish one 16½" side by turning under ¼" twice and top-stitching. Turn under 2¼" hem on one 18¼" side, turn under ¼" and blindstitch into place.

Lay 16" hemmed piece right-side-up on top of topstitched 16" piece, right-side-up, overlapping finished edges 4". This should create a finished opening to insert/remove pillow form in a 28" finished pillow back. Pin to hold in position.

Right sides together, sew pillow backing to ruffled pillow top, tucking ruffles in and out of the way, and sew ⅝" seam right on top of previous seams on pillow top. Sew all the way around. Trim corners. Turn right side out through finished pillow opening in middle of backing. Insert pillow form.

7. If you prefer, quilt the pillow top. After quilting, continue as above from Step #4.

Illus 88.

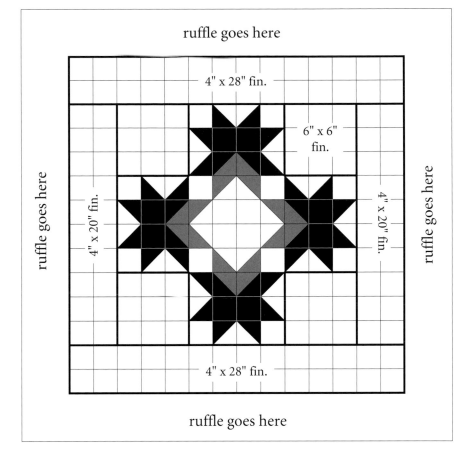

ruffle goes here

4" x 28" fin.

6" x 6" fin.

ruffle goes here

4" x 20" fin.

4" x 20" fin.

ruffle goes here

4" x 28" fin.

ruffle goes here

Pillow Piecing Diagram

Illus 89.

Pattern Templates

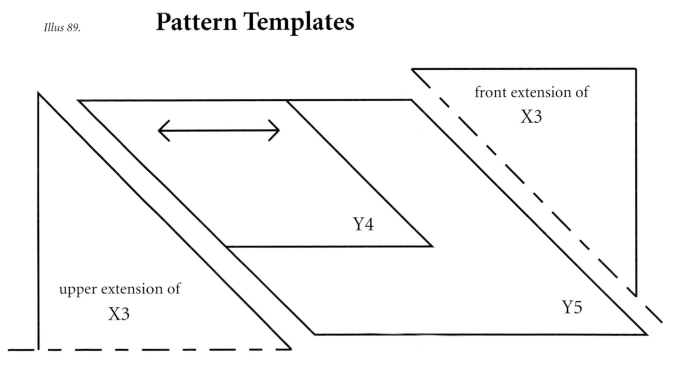

front extension of X3

Y4

upper extension of X3

Y5

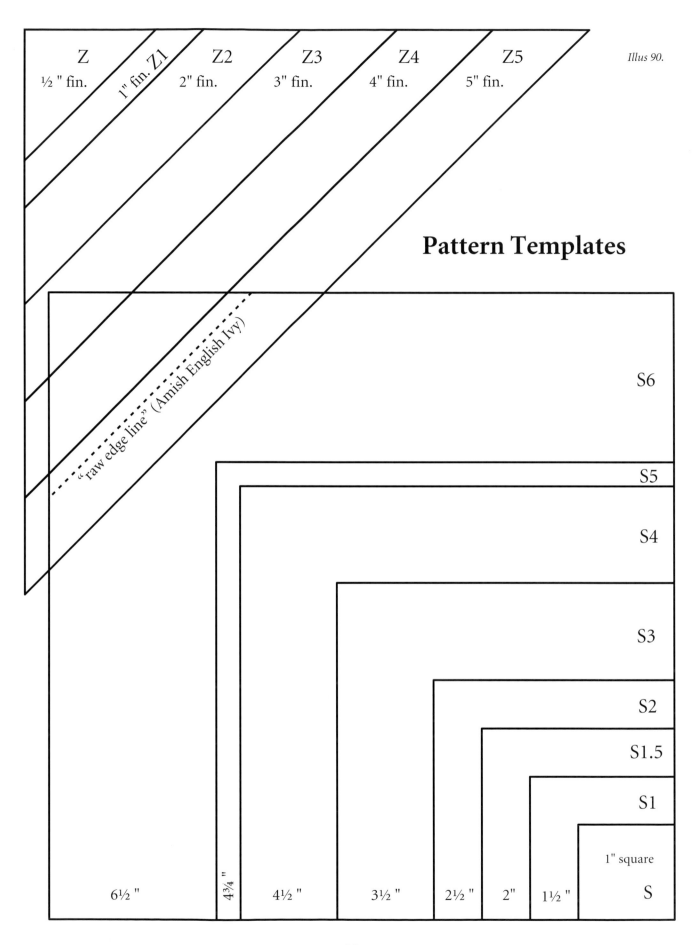

Z
½ " fin.

Z1
1" fin.

Z2
2" fin.

Z3
3" fin.

Z4
4" fin.

Z5
5" fin.

Illus 90.

Pattern Templates

"raw edge line" (Amish English Ivy)

S6

S5

S4

S3

S2

S1.5

S1

1" square

S

6½ "

4¾ "

4½ "

3½ "

2½ "

2"

1½ "

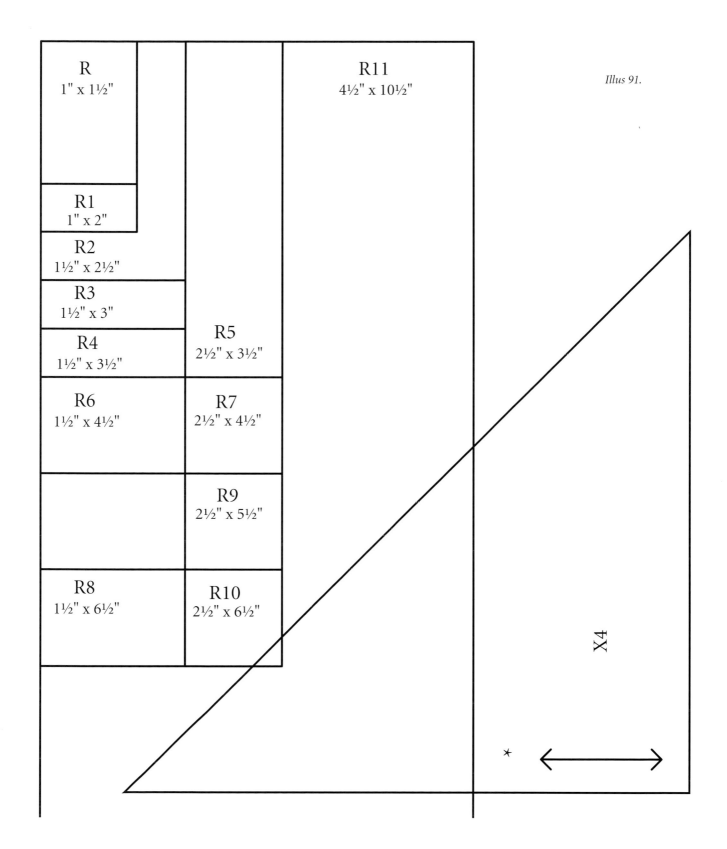

R
1" x 1½"

R11
4½" x 10½"

R1
1" x 2"

R2
1½" x 2½"

R3
1½" x 3"

R5
2½" x 3½"

R4
1½" x 3½"

R6
1½" x 4½"

R7
2½" x 4½"

R9
2½" x 5½"

R8
1½" x 6½"

R10
2½" x 6½"

X4

*

Due to paper size limitations, this template must be made longer.
It should measure 4½" x 10½".

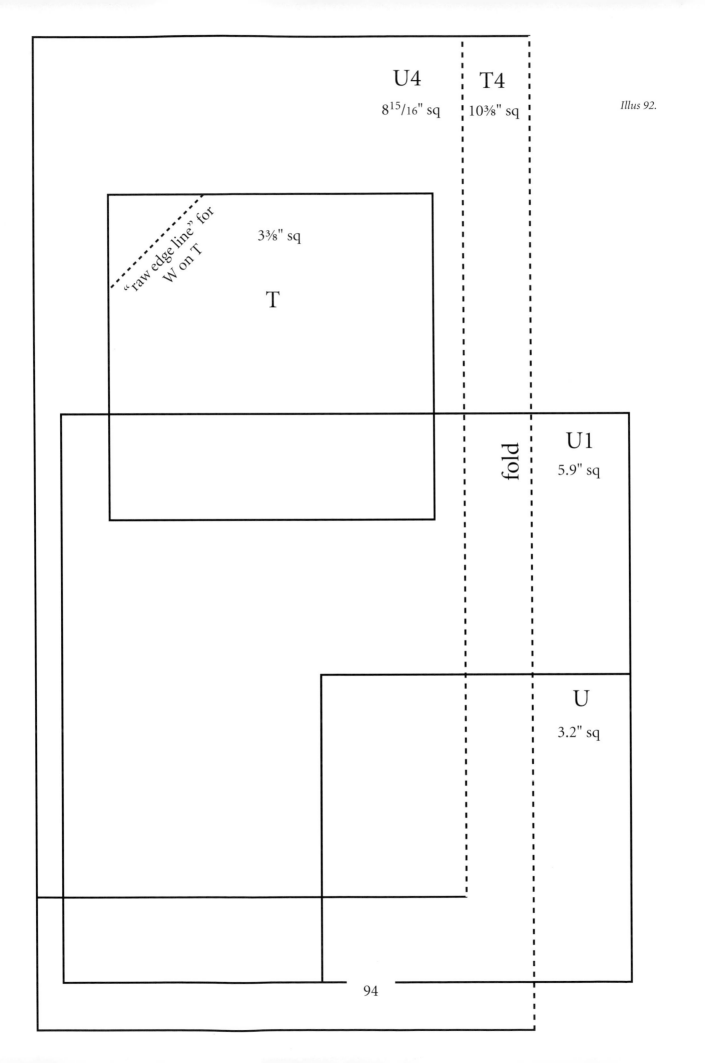

U4

8¹⁵/₁₆" sq

T4

10⅜" sq

Illus 92.

"raw edge line" for W on T

3⅜" sq

T

fold

U1

5.9" sq

U

3.2" sq

94

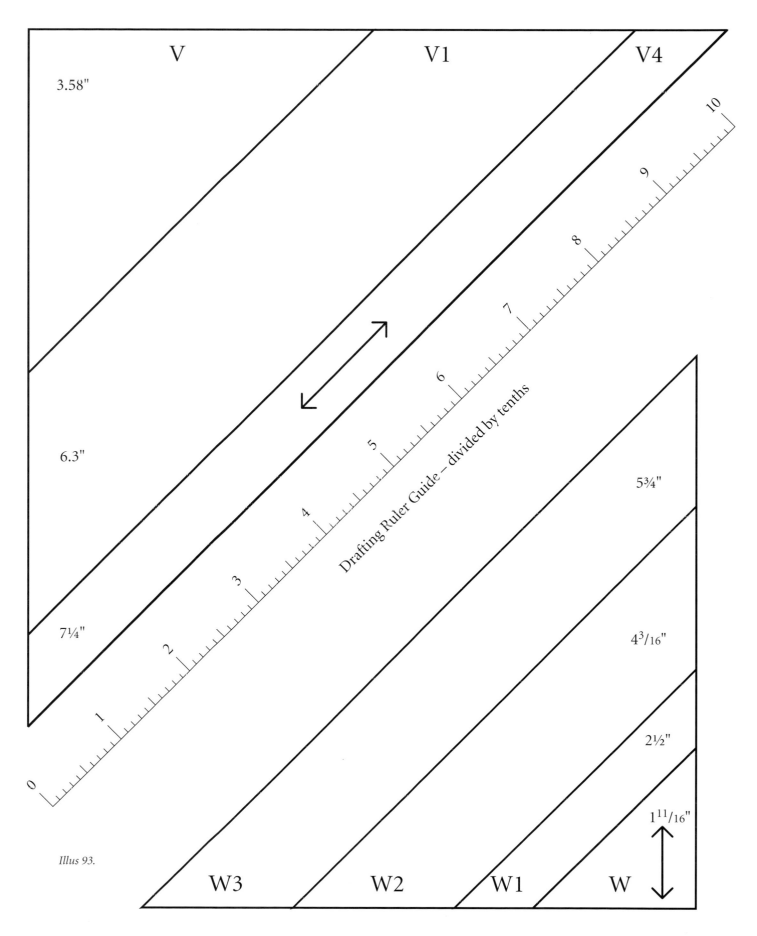

V

V1

V4

3.58"

10

9

8

7

6.3"

6

5

4

Drafting Ruler Guide – divided by tenths

5¾"

4³/₁₆"

7¼"

3

2

2½"

1

1¹¹/₁₆"

0

Illus 93.

W3

W2

W1

W

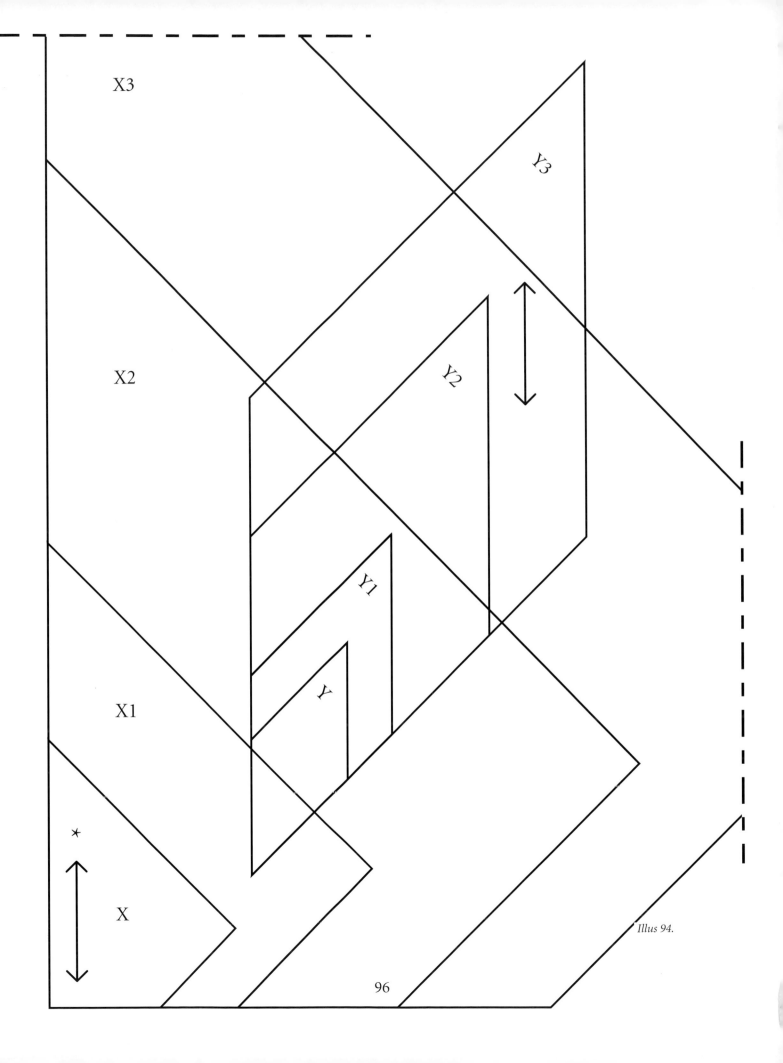

X3

Y3

X2

Y2

X1

Y1

Y

X

*

96

Illus 94.

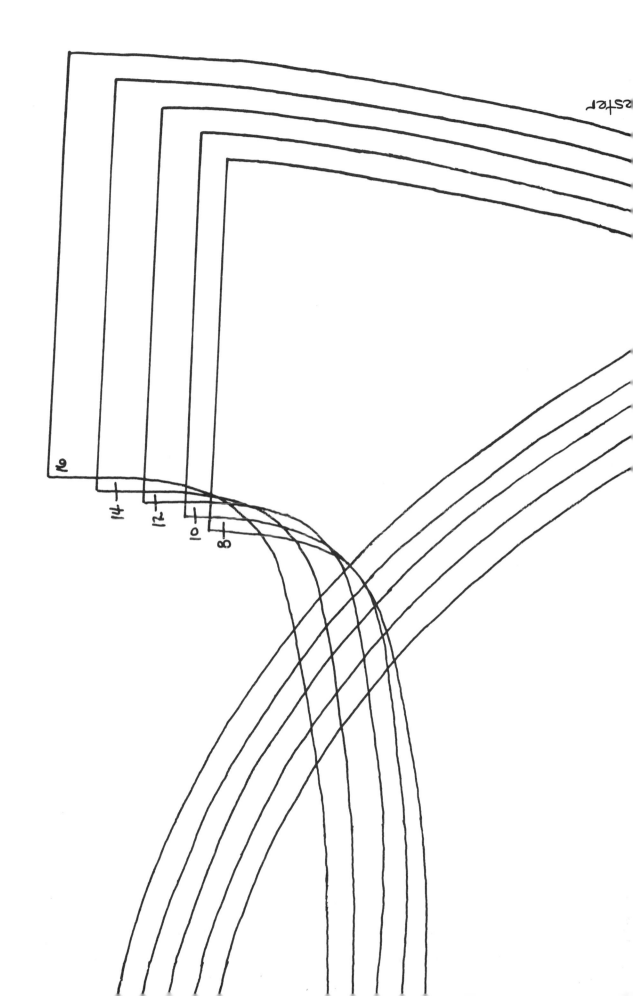

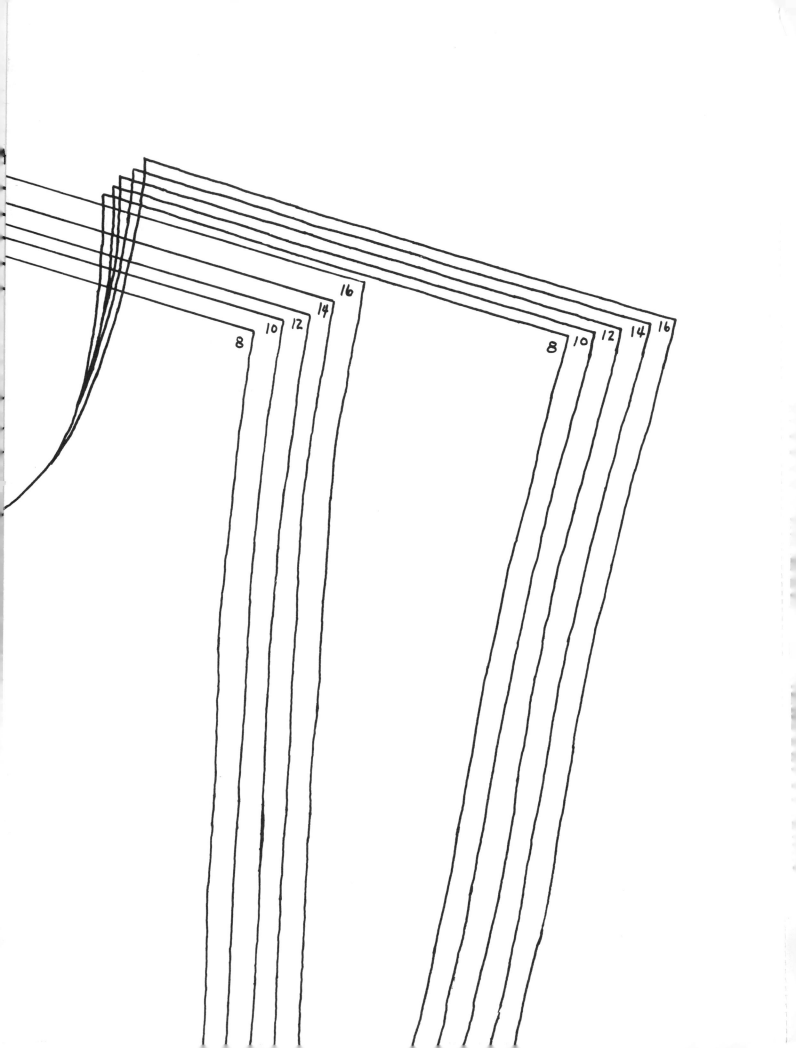